Heart Security

Safeguarding Your Redeemed Heart From The Inside Out

BY JESSICA D. MASON

Copyright © 2017 by Jessica D. Mason

Editing: Linda Gilden, Patrick Ragland, and Nonie Ratcliff
Interior Design: Pen to Print Publishing Services
Front Cover/Back Cover Design: Jessica D. Mason
Front Cover Art: Travis Fernatt and Michael Lynn Metcalf

The Library of Congress has cataloged *Heart Security*

ISBN-13: 978-0-69-287952-8
ISBN-10: 0-69-287952-8

*Unless otherwise notated, all scripture references are from the English Standard Translation

ABOUT THE AUTHOR

Jessica is a native of Lynchburg, VA but currently lives in Charlotte, NC. She holds her Bachelor of Arts in Music Education from Liberty University. For the past seven years, Jessica has consistently served with the non-profit organization, Agape Ambassadors Inc. This ministry shares the Gospel of Christ with incarcerated youth and unites volunteers of all backgrounds and ethnicities under the truth that "Jesus is the Answer." Jessica's faithful service to this ministry has birthed her own revelation of who she is in Christ, her passions, and her own heart for other young women to know Jesus Christ as their hearts' treasure.

Jessica is also a traumatic brain injury survivor and experienced God's miraculous healing and power. She began writing and speaking about her injury and Christ's healing power through mentoring teen girls and moms in a ministry she founded called, Sweet Meet. Her message of *Heart Security* became a resource she used in sharing how a heart that solely worships Christ, is a heart of sustaining power and influence.

Besides writing Jessica is a public speaker and accepts speaking engagements to share her testimony and encourage young women to deepen in their relationship with Christ. She is also a recording artist and the lead vocalist in the group, Graft3d, that she and her brother started in 2016. You can find Graft3d's single, "Come to Praise," on iTunes, CD Baby, or Amazon.

ACKNOWLEDGEMENTS

Thank you Lord Jesus for your faithfulness to me and giving me this honor to share with the world just a portion of what you have shared with me. My heart is yours because you've paid the highest price for it. Thank you.

Mom. What can I say? You are definitely a rock in my life and I appreciate your love, support, and listening ear. Thank you for teaching me the importance of being "set apart." I love you and am excited to tackle many more adventures with you.

I also want to shout out to you Dad. You keep me on my toes. Thank you for all the wisdom, advise, and fishing trips. Thanks for the laughs and being such an awesome provider, community leader, minister, and defender. You make me feel safe in this unpredictable world.

To the best brother for me, DJ. Thank you for encouraging me to just be me. Thank you for always being there. You know? You have reflected the grace of God to me so many times. I look up to you even though you're my little brother. You've got the light man! Keep letting Jesus shine through you!

Grandma Edna! I'm your "Little Woman" forever and always and I want to say I love you, thank you for absolutely EVERYTHING, and spending these 31 years with you has been treasured gifts. Muah!

Oh Amber! The laughs, the cries, the challenges, the tough love, the Chick-fil-A trips, the hiking trips gone wrong, the words of encouragement on a daily basis……. Thanks Sis!

To Pop, Grandad Edward, Grandma Ollie, Aunties, Uncles, Cuzzos, friends and other family who have been there through it all; you know who you are……. I love you and thank you for loving on me and making me feel as though I matter. Thank you for the prayers, support, tutoring, the hairdos, the time spent, the mechanic work, the detailing, the pizza, the pool time, and the movie nights! Thank you!

Thank you Blue Ridge Writers Conference friends for your advice and encouragement. To Linda, Patrick, Travis, Michael, and Nonie, thank you for investing your talent and services to this message. Lastly, big thanks to you. Thank you for purchasing the book, and pressing your way through the journey of securing your Redeemed Heart. May God richly bless you all.

TABLE OF CONTENTS

Introduction: Welcome to Heart Security

Have you ever been hoodwinked by a con artist, lied to by a salesman, or had something dear to you stolen? Being deceived, falsely accused, and robbed are three things that really stink! It can leave your heart feeling ashamed, angry, sad, and even calloused. Even though we have received Jesus Christ as our Lord and Savior, and the Holy Spirit is living in us, we still can find our heart's affection drawn away from the Lord to the deceitful pleasures of this world. The Prince of Evil is just waiting to make his move. Why do we even have to deal with such horrible things in life? Is there any way we can keep our hearts from being captured by the Father of Lies, the Master of Deception, and the #1 Thief?

This book will help you strategically guard your heart from the inside out. The Lord gave me the idea for *Heart Security* while I was recovering from a traumatic brain injury. During my recovery, the Holy Spirit used the Word of God to show me practical ways to stay in faith and move deeper into my relationship with Christ. It was my relationship with Jesus Christ and the promises of His word that protected my heart from false hope, depression, hopelessness, and fear. Standing on the Word of God was the catalyst for a miraculous recovery.

Even though God did so many amazing things in my life, sometimes fear and doubt still crept into my heart. Hebrews 11:6 tells us that without faith it's impossible to please God. We must feed our faith by hearing the Word of God, so we can move without limitation in the things of God. Our faith allows us to have the things God says He has given us through Christ, and this starts with guarding our hearts. As we move through this curriculum, be honest with our Lord Jesus. Use the Take It to Heart activities to really reflect on the Word of God and what it has to say about your own personal affections.

Don't be afraid to allow the Holy Spirit to correct you and put you on paths of righteousness. The Lord disciplines us because He loves us, and our desire should be that He is the central affection of our hearts (Hebrews 12:6, Matthew 22:37–39).

Keeping our best love toward Him overflows into the rest of our lives, giving us the abundant life He came to give to us (John 10:10). You and I should always remember that Jesus Christ living in us is the ultimate security for our hearts. His Spirit inside of us is greater than the evil in the world. We can't take for granted that there is an enemy that still wants to infect our hearts with evil and cause us to move in paths that are harmful to our lives and detrimental to the purpose God has for us. We can participate in keeping our hearts safe from this enemy by protecting the affections of our hearts. This book will help you acknowledge God's love for us through his Son Jesus and show how we can nourish our heart's affection for Him. You will see how harmful agents try to penetrate our heart's defenses and cause us to set up idols in our hearts. You will begin to understand the armor God has given us to protect our hearts against spiritual weapons that come our way.

We will refer to Proverbs 4:23 frequently. The Living Bible translation says, "Above all else, guard your affections. For they influence everything else in your life." In the King James Version, this same verse reads, "Keep thy heart with all diligence; for out of it are the issues of life." What are affections, really? The definition of affection is, "a feeling of liking or caring for someone or something" (Merriam-Webster.com). Let's stop and take this verse to heart.

TAKE IT TO HEART

This activity is designed to help you detect the affections of your own heart. As you're writing out your affections, ask yourself these questions:

   a. Who or what do I think about FIRST when I wake up in the morning?

   b. Who or what do I turn to FIRST when I need help?

   c. Who or what brings me the most excitement during my day?

d. What do I spend most of my time doing?

e. Who do I talk to the most?

f. Who or what do I love the most?

g. Who or what are my thoughts centered around? What kinds of thoughts do I have?

This is just an example of how your heart may look:

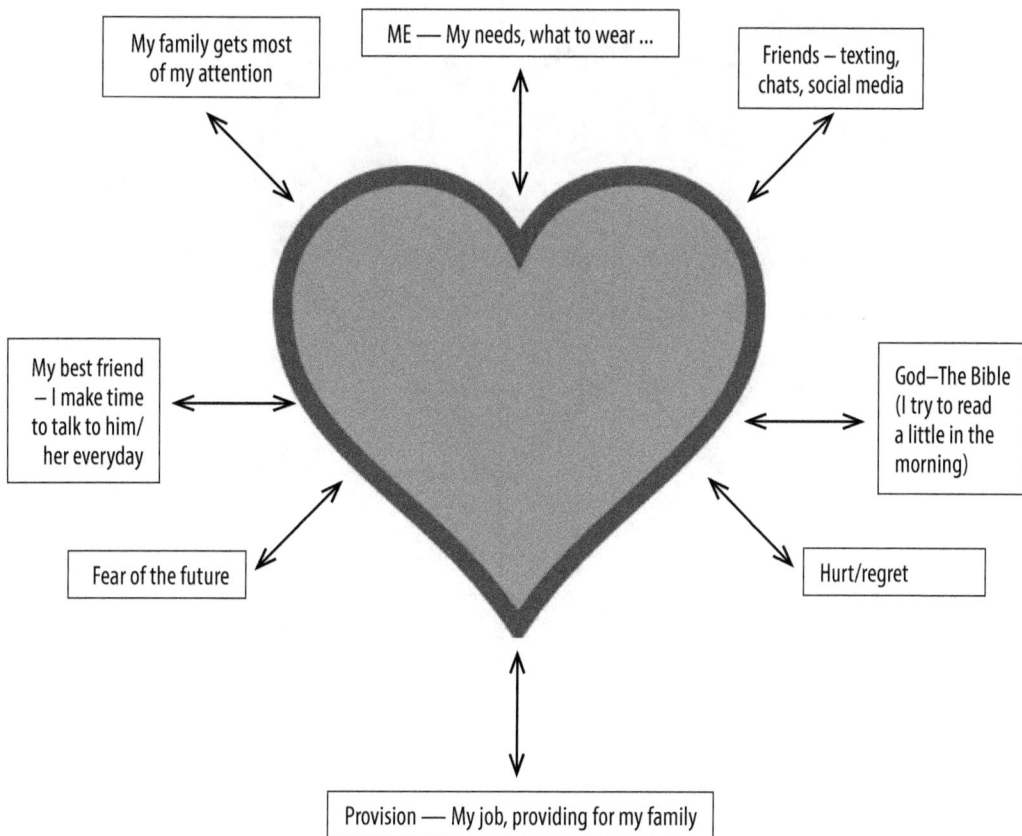

My family gets most of my attention

ME — My needs, what to wear …

Friends – texting, chats, social media

My best friend – I make time to talk to him/ her everyday

God–The Bible (I try to read a little in the morning)

Fear of the future

Hurt/regret

Provision — My job, providing for my family

Now it's YOUR turn. Use colored pencils or markers and write out each affection in a different color.

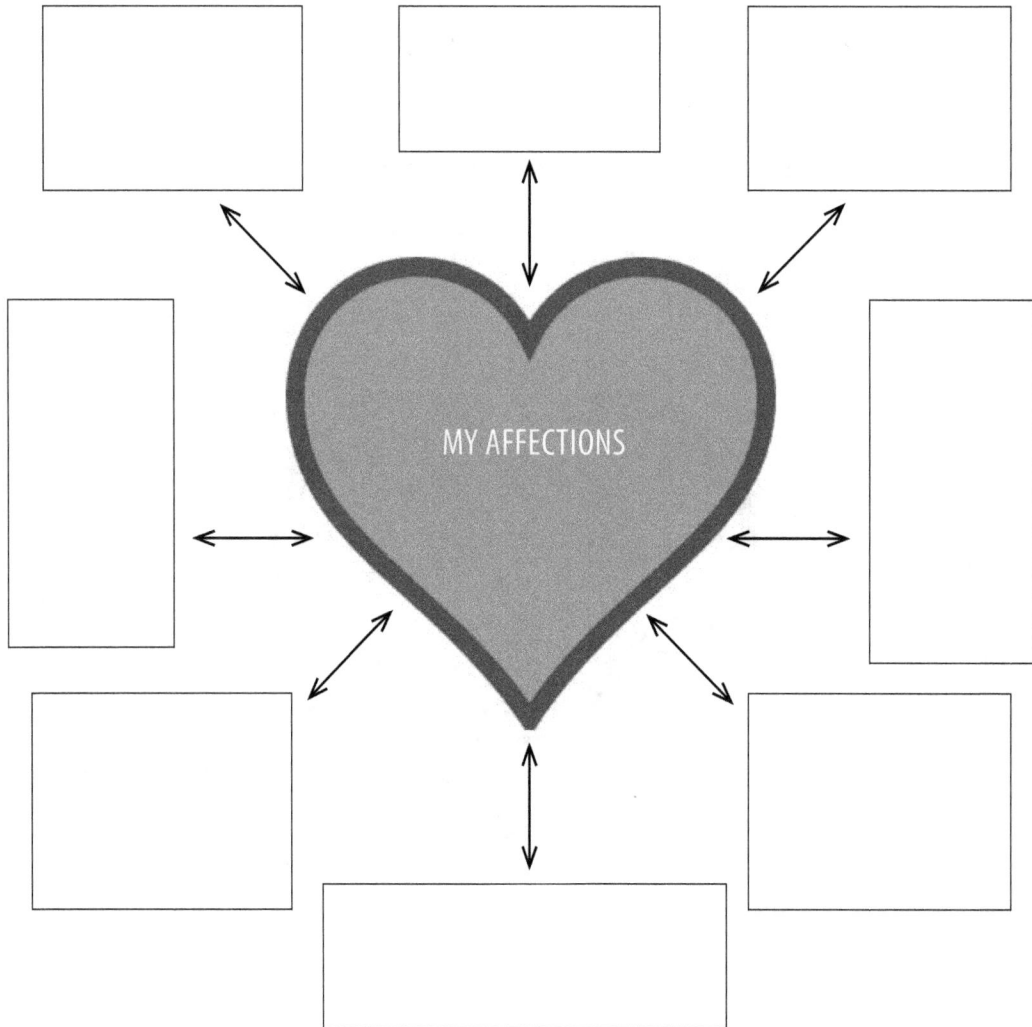

MY AFFECTIONS

Take another look at your heart. If you're doing this activity with a study group, share your heart with others. Make sure you LISTEN to the hearts of others. Remember not to judge or criticize. Listen with ears of LOVE.

Look at what's in your heart, consider the following questions: Are your affections, attention, and thoughts Christ-centered and rooted in love? Is someone or something else the center of your heart?

According to John J. Parsons, the Hebrew word for "issues" is *totz'ot* (Parsons, "Keep thy Heart"*)*. Parsons says *totz'ot* literally refers to the borders or boundaries of an area. He further explains that Proverbs 4:23 is saying your heart produces a map or chart to your life. In closing, he states, "How you choose to guard your heart from the corruption and hardness of the world will determine the 'road' of your life" (Parsons, "Keep thy Heart").

God gives us Proverbs 4:23 to reveal to us the secret to life. The condition of our hearts affect the quality of our lives. Think about it. Your physical heart is the central organ of your body. It pumps blood to all of your organs. Leviticus 17:11 tells us that the "life of the flesh is in the blood." It is common knowledge that without a healthy heart, you will live an unhealthy life that will likely result in an untimely death. The same is true with our *spiritual* hearts.

God did not originally create us with a "sin-diseased" heart. If you take a look back in Genesis, you will find God created male and female in His image and said they were good. He said that *everything* He made was good. When Adam, the first man, disobeyed God, sin entered the world and caused our hearts to no longer be the perfect, healthy, righteous hearts God intended (Genesis 3). Instead, we got deceitful, desperately wicked hearts (Jeremiah 17:9) that desire and lust after evil (1 John 2:16, James 1:14). These sin-sick hearts became hardened to the voice of God because they were so waxed over by sin that it was nearly impossible to respond in obedience to God. Our waxed-over hearts inhibit us from a relationship with God because God is Holy and will judge sin; not fellowship with it. Our hearts desperately need a Savior to peel that wax off and create in us a clean heart and renew in us a right spirit (Psalm 51:10). Who is able to peel off the waxy sin of our hearts? Who is able to soften our hearts and empower us to love God completely with all our hearts, souls, minds, and strengths? Who is able to empower our hearts to love our neighbors as we love ourselves? (Matthew 22:37–40)

You may already know and have experienced the answer to these questions, but whether you know or you're not sure, I believe everyone can benefit from this book. My hope is that you are encouraged, enlightened, and empowered as we unravel the ultimate security plan for your heart. I don't know about you, but I'm excited, so let's jump right in!

Maximum Level Security

I was around 20 years old when I started going into juvenile detention facilities with my parents. Their ministry, Agape Ambassadors, Inc., was faithful in going in and sharing the Gospel with the kids in this type of facility. I have to say that I wasn't so excited about going into a jail, even if it was designed for the underage, so I was lukewarm in my commitment until the age of 24. Once I started going on a regular basis, I became more and more familiar with how the facility operated, and I became more comfortable with the security measures the staff took to ensure the kids' safety, as well as my own. In preparing for a lesson about loving the Lord with all your heart, and safeguarding that love, the "D-home" came to mind. The Holy Spirit began to enlighten me on how the security measures in the jail are very similar to how we should guard our hearts against sin and Satan. Now, all facilities are not the same, and each one has its own unique way of securing the inmates from outside threats as well as breakouts from the inside. I'm simply using the facility I frequently visit to give us a general picture of this thing called Heart Security.

Our central verse is going to be Proverbs 4:23, but before we even come close to a Security Plan, we are going to take our time to lay a foundation. There are some important questions we need answered when it comes to the heart, so we'll start with these: What is the heart? Why are we securing it? Who are we guarding it from?

What Is the Heart?

*Proverbs 4:23 "Keep your heart with all vigilance,
for from it flow the springs of life." (English Standard Version)*

What do you think of when I say "heart"?

Take some space here and write down words that come to mind…..

_____

_____

_____

_____

Proverbs 23:7 says, "For as he thinks in his heart, so is he" (Amplified Bible).

In Matthew 15:17–20, Jesus comes along and explains to His disciples:

"Do you not see that whatever goes into the mouth passes into the stomach and is expelled? But what comes out of the mouth proceeds from the heart, and this defiles a person. For out of the heart come evil thoughts, murder, adultery, sexual immorality, theft, false witness, slander. These are what defile a person. But to eat with unwashed hands does not defile anyone."

Our hearts are more than the platform of our love for someone or our passion for something. *The Jewish Encyclopedia* states that the heart is the seat of our feelings, intellect, and will. It houses the belief system which develops your identity (Kohler, et al.). What we allow inside our eye and ear gates enters our thoughts, and if we think…and think…and think…. Those thoughts seep into our hearts and graft into our identity.

That is why God commanded Joshua to meditate on His Word both day and night so that he would have success. Meditation is thinking….and thinking…..and thinking…..as well as mumbling the Word of God under your breath. It seeps into your heart and develops your identity. Romans 12:1–2 tells us the Word of God renews our mind: It changes our thinking!

Take a look back at what Jesus says in Matthew 15:8: "*The things that come out of a person's mouth come from the heart.*"

This verse makes me think of the saying "You are what you eat," and here Jesus is introducing the root of the matter: You are what you THINK. Take a look back at verse 19: "for out of the heart comes evil THOUGHTS." (emphasis added).

I love this conversation in The Message translation:

> [15]Peter said, "I don't get it. Put it in plain language."

> [16–20]Jesus replied, "You, too? Are you being willfully stupid? Don't you know that anything that is swallowed works its way through the intestines and is finally defecated? But what comes out of the mouth gets its start in the heart. It's from the heart that we vomit up evil arguments, murders, adulteries, fornications, thefts, lies, and cussing. That's what pollutes. Eating or not eating certain foods, washing or not washing your hands—that's neither here nor there."

If I were to write out this verse into a conversation between Jesus and me; it might look like this....

Jesus: So, Jessica, are you serious? Do you really believe that what you think about doesn't matter?

Me: Well, I haven't given it much thought. LOL. No pun intended. No, seriously, Jesus. I don't really see how my thought life has anything to do with the kind of person I am. Now that you mention it, though, I guess you're right. I do see how I care more about the food I'm eating than what I think about.

Jesus: Let me be the one to tell you: Your thoughts matter. You think you are the bomb dot com because you exercise and try to make healthy choices to have a wonderful-looking body? What's that got to do with your heart? Let me ask you something: If your body looked like what your heart looks like, would you be happy?

Me: Wow. What a tough question. I'm not sure. I would hope so.

Jesus: When you gossip, judge others unfairly, and say mean things in anger, it just doesn't come out of your mouth from nowhere. Whatever is lodged in your heart will most definitely come out of your mouth, and your thoughts affect the condition of your heart.

Me: Lord, I'm sorry. Please forgive me. Help me to think on good things so that my heart will pour out of my mouth Your words and not words that harm.

Proverbs 4:23 is such an important verse because it tells us to GUARD our hearts ABOVE anything else! When we guard are hearts we are guarding our very identities!

Read these scriptures on the importance of your thoughts:

2 Corinthians 10:5 (ESV)
We destroy arguments and every lofty opinion raised against the knowledge of God, and take every thought captive to obey Christ.

Colossians 3:2–5 (ESV)
Set your minds on things that are above, not on things that are on earth. For you have died, and your life is hidden with Christ in God. When Christ who is your life appears, then you also will appear with him in glory.

Put to death therefore what is earthly in you: sexual immorality, impurity, passion, evil desire, and covetousness, which is idolatry.

Philippians 4:4–8 (ESV)
Rejoice in the Lord always; again I will say, rejoice. Let your reasonableness be known to everyone. The Lord is at hand; do not be anxious about anything, but in everything by prayer and supplication with thanksgiving let your requests be made known to God. And the peace of God, which surpasses all understanding, *will guard your hearts and your minds* in Christ Jesus (emphasis added).

Finally, brothers, whatever is true, whatever is honorable, whatever is just, whatever is pure, whatever is lovely, whatever is commendable, if there is any excellence, if there is anything worthy of praise, think about these things.

MESSAGES ➡ THOUGHTS ➡ YOU

(social media, TV, false doctrine,

music, friends, pastors, teachers,

co-workers, etc.)

The contents of your heart has a lot to do with what kinds of messages you are allowing in your ear and eye gates. What are you listening to? Who are you listening to? What are you reading? What are you watching?

Reflection

Let's Review...

What is the heart?

1. Our hearts are the control room of our souls.

2. Our hearts are the factory of our identity.

> *Proverbs 4:23 "Keep (guard) your heart with all diligence*
> *for out of it springs the issues (course) of life."*

We've got our first question answered! Our hearts house our belief systems. Our thoughts, actions and words are the three components of our identities and all get their start from our heart. That's why it's extremely important to take Philippians 4:8 to heart and guard what we think about.

But is that all? Is it that simple? If you think good things, you'll have a good heart?

Take a moment to think or discuss…. (Make sure you use Scripture to justify your answers). Write you answers in the space below.

_____

_____

_____

_____

_____

Just thinking good thoughts can't change our own hearts from wicked to righteous. God is the standard of good, and on our own we fall short every time. That's why we must put our trust in Jesus to change our hearts. Why? He is the only one who can.

Why Are We Guarding Our Hearts?

Proverbs 4:23 "Keep (guard) your heart with all diligence
for out of it springs the issues (course) of life."

We've skimmed the surface of what our hearts are; the control room of our soul and the factory of our identity. Now let's focus on why our hearts are so valuable.

I've had my 2000 Dodge Neon for 10 years. It's my baby because I got that car by faith! I'm serious. I was in college, my Honda broke down, and finding rides to class and work was driving me up the wall. I was trusting God for this 2003 Toyota Camry that was way out of my budget, but my prayer was that God would move on the seller's heart and bring the price into my budget range. This was a leap of faith, because I was offering $10,000 less than what he was asking. No, you read it right. I was offering him $2,000 for the car.

To my surprise, he kept calling me back trying to negotiate payment plans, prices and the like. My dad thought it was very skeptical that this man was calling me back if the car was worth what he said it was, so he told me about a guy at his job selling his Dodge and wanted to know if I would take a look at it. Well, I ended up loving the car, and it was in my price range. God provided!

Years later, I took the car to have it inspected, and when I got it back, the mechanic had cut the wires to my passenger side mirror and completely taken the mirror off. The automotive shop had cut the wires to my fog lights and completely taken them out just because the bulbs had blown. When I got my car back, anger was an understatement. My car had been abused! My baby had been unrightfully stripped, and there wasn't much I could do about it. AAAGGHHH! I felt like crying, giving those people a piece of my mind, and screaming. I actually did do a little screaming. The point is, something that was precious to me and had sentimental value was damaged and defiled by people who could care less.

Now, we are SO much more valuable to God than an old car, but I wonder how God felt when Satan lied, Eve was deceived, Adam disobeyed, and sin was free to have his way with the beautiful children God had created in His own image. I wonder if the Creator, the Father of Lights, the Almighty felt any of the emotions I felt when He looked at *the hearts of his precious babies and noticed the wires that were directly connected to Him had been severed.*

TAKE IT TO HEART

Think about something you really care about or treasure. Write down or discuss how you would feel if your treasure was marred or stolen by someone.

Now think about someone you really love. How would you feel if the relationship just ended? How would you feel if that person dropped you and ran toward someone who you know will only do them harm?

That's exactly what happened in the Garden of Eden. God created us to have a relationship with Him. In John 15:14, Jesus says, "You are my friends if you do what I command."

We see in the garden that this friendship went out the window when Adam and Eve did the opposite of what God commanded.

Look at this verse: "For by him all things were created, in heaven and on earth, visible and invisible, whether thrones or dominions or rulers or authorities—all things were created through him and for him" (Colossians 1:16).

What do you notice?

In this verse, who is the Creator? ("…by Him all things were created…")

_____

_____

Back up and read Colossians chapter 1 verses 1–18. You'll see that Paul is clearly talking about Christ. Take a look at verse 17:

> *"And He is before all things, and in Him all things consist."*

Not only did Christ create, but He is the one who sustains and upholds everything that He has made. EVERYTHING! All things in heaven and earth, visible and invisible! He made it all and He holds it all—even our hearts.

What was God's intention for creating us? Our hearts?

Isaiah 43:7:

> *"Everyone who is called by my name. Whom I have created for My glory;*
> *I have formed him, yes, I have made him."*

Do you see the answer?

For HIS glory! He created you and your heart for His glory!

What does that mean? It sounds important, right? It sounds like we are pretty valuable. Well, you're right! We are valuable, and anything valuable is worth guarding! Wouldn't you agree?

In Genesis 2:7, we read that God breathed the breath of life into the dust man He created. When He did, that man became a living being.

This living being came with a heart. According to the *NAS Exhaustive Concordance*, heart in Hebrew is *lebab*, which means "the inner man, mind, will, heart."

What was God's original intention for giving this dust man life with a heart in his inner parts?

Can you imagine? Let's slow down a little and *take it to heart*. You'll need some Play-Doh.

1. Genesis says that God made man in His image, male and female. Take some Play-Doh and make a figure in "your own image." Make your Play-Doh figure a representation of you!

2. Think about or share what it is about this figure that reminds you of who you are.

3. Look at your creation: What's missing? It's missing LIFE! It doesn't have a heart that can respond to you, love you, or choose to obey you.

4. Blow into your creation's nostrils and pretend that it has come to life. Share with your group or write down what you would like the heart of your creation to be like. In order to fully answer this question, you may need to ask yourself why you made him/her in the first place?

5. Why do you think God made us?

6. What do you think God intended for our hearts to be like toward Him?

As Adam looked around at the beautiful garden God had made for him, God gave him a command:

"You are free to eat from any tree in the garden; but you must not eat from the tree of the knowledge of good and evil, for when you eat from it you will certainly die" (Genesis 2:16–17).

God has just given Adam *life* because He is *life* and now He is telling Adam how to preserve the *life* he has been given. The first thing God instructs Adam on is how to guard his heart. He is now a LIVING being, which means he has a physical heart and a spiritual heart. He has God's very breath, making him a living being that has an inner man.

We are the only created beings in the universe that are made in the image of God! God didn't just create you; He fashioned you in His Image for His glory!

God formed us, through Christ, so that His greatness, presence, brightness, character, and salvation power can be seen. I heard someone explain it like this: We are God's magnifying glass. Our very beings, the way we were made, formed, divinely and intricately put together magnifies who God is so that He gets all the praise, glory, honor, and credit. We are walking, talking, living, loving, and breathing proof that God indeed gets all the credit for life. He gets the credit for everything in heaven and earth; what is seen and not seen; powers, thrones, and authorities. We are his workmanship. The very work of His own hands: "*For we are his workmanship, created in Christ Jesus for good works, which God prepared beforehand, that we should walk in them.*" (Ephesians 2:10 ESV)

That's not all! In Ephesians 3:9–10 Paul reveals it was God's intention to call everyone who believes in Jesus Christ by His own name. Calling us by His name means we belong to Him. Everyone is God's creation, but not everyone belongs to God. Only those who believe in His Son Jesus Christ and trust only Him to save them from their sin belong to God. That means if you are a believer in Jesus Christ and have asked him to forgive you of all sin and give you a brand new heart, Christ lives in your heart (Ephesians 3:17). Then, you belong to God, are in the family of God, and are empowered to reflect the GLORY of God! Jesus living in your heart gives you the capacity to experience the very presence of God and be completely filled with God Himself. (Go ahead. Read all of Ephesians 3.)

In Christ, you carry the very presence of God. From top to bottom, you are full of God's glory. Christ lives in your heart when you invite him in by faith which is *why* we are guarding our hearts.

We guard our hearts because they are the home of the Creator that made it, the Christ who rescued it from sin, and the place where God floods His perfect love and the fullness of His presence in and through our beings and our lives.

Why? It's important for you to guard your heart because of who's in it: the Almighty God, Creator of Heaven and Earth, your Redeemer—Jesus Christ. When Jesus lives in your heart, He comes in and melts the sinful wax off your wicked, deceitful heart. He applies His blood and washes your heart white as snow. You become a brand new creature. All old things pass away, and all things become new (2 Corinthians 5:17).

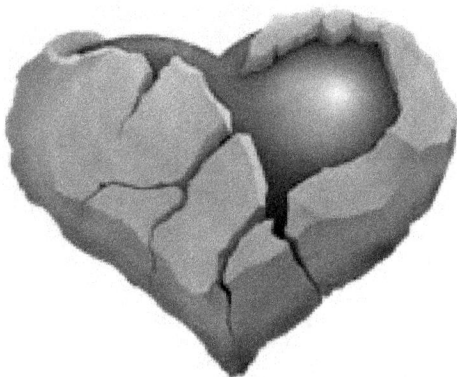

Jesus comes in and lives in your nice, clean heart. When His Spirit is in there, your heart is softened to the things of God, the Word of God, and the move of God. Jesus makes you right with God so that you can enjoy fellowship with God.

Only Jesus can do that. Remember, He says in John 14:6, "I am the way, the truth, and the life. No man comes to the Father but by me." Wow! Let's take this to heart

TAKE IT TO HEART

Have you ever asked Jesus Christ to forgive you of your sins and come live in your heart? If so, when and where?

_____

_____

_____

If not, would you like to? Stop right here and say this prayer with me.

Lord Jesus,

I admit I am a sinner. I realize that because I have a sin nature I am separated from you. I don't want a wax covered heart anymore. Thank you for the blood you shed on the cross for my sins. Please forgive me of all my sin. I confess with my mouth that Jesus is Lord, and I believe in my heart that God has raised you from the dead. I ask that you come into my heart and make me a brand new creation. I will no longer be the boss of my own life. You are my boss, my Lord, and my Savior. Thank you for making your home in my heart because of my confession of faith in you. Thank you for sealing me with the Holy Spirit and sending Him to be my comforter and guide. Thank you that I have now been born into the family of God.

A-men

If you just prayed that prayer you have taken the first and most important step in safe-guarding your heart. You have eternal life through Jesus Christ! Hallelujah! You are set free from the strongholds of sin and death. You have been given abundant life and are now my brother/sister in Christ. Congratulations and Happy Birthday! Please let me know if you received Christ as your savior. Email me at guardmyheart4u@gmail.com. I want to personally congratulate you into the Kingdom.

If Jesus lives in your heart, how has He changed the way you think, speak, and act? Why or why not?

_____

_____

_____

Are there any relationships in your life that are better now because Jesus is in your heart?

_____

_____

_____

Does knowing Jesus died for your sins change your perspective about participating in sin? Why or why not?

_____

_____

_____

What are some ways that you protect your precious relationship with Jesus now that He lives in your heart?

_____

_____

_____

_____

Do you know anyone who has not asked Jesus to be their Lord and Savior and live in their heart? Commit to praying for that person this week and ask Jesus to give you an opportunity to share how you were before your relationship with Christ, how you met Christ, and how He changed your heart.

Practice here:

My Testimony

Before I had a relationship with Christ, I was (describe yourself before Salvation) …

_____

_____

_____

I asked forgiveness for my sins and confessed Jesus as Lord (describe when, where, how) …

_____

_____

After Christ came into my heart, I (describe yourself today as a result of Christ in your life) …

_____

_____

_____

Proverbs 4:23 "Keep (guard) your heart with all diligence
for out of it springs the issues (course) of life."

Who Are We Guarding Our Hearts From?

John 14:6 says Jesus is the Way, the Truth, and the Life.

Many verses explain that Jesus is Life, He created Life, and He is the giver of Life.

John 1:1–3 says, *In the beginning was the Word, and the Word was with God, and the Word was God. He was in the beginning with God. All things came into being through Him, and apart from Him nothing came into being that has come into being.*

Now read these verses out loud:

Genesis 1:1–2
In the beginning God created the heavens and the earth. The earth was formless and void, and darkness was over the surface of the deep, and the Spirit of God was moving over the surface of the waters.

Nehemiah 9:6
You alone are the LORD. You made the heavens, even the highest heavens, and all their starry host, the earth and all that is on it, the seas and all that is in them. You give life to everything, and the multitudes of heaven worship you.

We see that Jesus is God. Yes, He is the Son of God, meaning He is the only sinless human being with God's own divine nature, but He is also God in flesh. John lets us in on the deity of Jesus by introducing Him as "The Word" who created all things in the beginning: "….and the Word was God…."

Jesus is Life and He created you and me. He gave us Life!

This life that God gave us came with a GPS system. Do you see it in our central verse?

Proverbs 4:23 "Keep (guard) your heart with all diligence for out of it springs the issues (course) of life."

Remember what Mr. Parson said earlier: Our hearts draw a map for our lives. In other words, our hearts create the course, the direction, the boundary, the map of our life.

WHOA!

From whom or what do you think your heart needs protecting? Our life is valuable because it came from God, and your heart is powerful because the course of your life comes from it. So who or what would want to tamper with your heart?

I'll give you a hint: Who is God's number-one enemy? Well, if God loves you, then His number-one enemy is your number-one enemy.

I'm really big on action movies. I mean the ones that involve the hero and the villain. You know: *Superman*, *Spider Man*, *The Flash*, etc. Have you ever noticed that the whole hero-villain storyline is the same? The villain finds out who the hero loves most and targets them to get to the heart of the hero. Wow! They really got this motif from the Bible.

Satan's strategy is to get to the heart of God. How? John 3:16: "For God so loved the world that he gave his only begotten Son." We are the heart of God. God loves us. God loves you. His love for us is so strong that He gave the only Son He had to die for us, so that we would be able to live with Him forever. It's a crazy love, a love that compelled Him to wrap Himself in flesh and live among us for 33 years. It's an out-of-this-world kind of love. Satan knows the only way to cause God pain is to deceive us. If he can get to our hearts and cause us to turn away from the relationship Jesus so desperately wants to have with us—well, you get the picture.

Security Plan for the Heart

As I have mentioned, my family has a non-profit organization called Agape Ambassadors Inc. We go into the Juvenile Detention facilities and introduce the kids to Jesus. We have summer retreats called, "Jesus is the Answer," that overshadow the kids with the love of Christ. The facilities we enter have a security plan in place and

I want to use the way they secure the kids as an illustration of how we are to guard our hearts.

Let's first look at the entrance.

When we arrive at the facility, the first security measure is the entrance. You can't just walk into a jail. There is a locked door, and you have to ring the bell and identify yourself. A *security list* is used to determine whether or not you gain access. If your name isn't on that list, you cannot enter the building. If you try to enter without access you will find yourself "taken captive" by the authorities.

Do you see where we're going with this?

Your heart is like this facility. It holds your faith and GPS that maps the course of your life. The juvenile detention holds children that have been incarcerated, but the hope is that their lives will change and their courses will turn for the better.

So how does the locked door and the entrance relate to guarding your heart?

The Entrance

The locked door represents your eyes and ears.

Our hearts are greatly affected by what we think. Thoughts are greatly affected by the messages we receive through what we hear and see in the world around us.

1 John 2:16 says,
For all that is in the world, the lust of the flesh and the *lust of the eyes* and the boastful pride of life, is not from the Father, but is from the world.

Lust of the eye in our terminology could mean, "I want it because I see it and I'll do anything to get it."

Does our society embrace or reject this way of thinking?

It EMBRACES IT! WHY? Because of money. The commercial industry is huge in America. Companies know if they make a product or an ideal look good, then most likely people will buy it.

The Bible enlightens us that this is not new. God understands that when we look at things that attract us, whether it be sexually, emotionally or psychologically our sinful nature tends to desire it. It is no secret that our society idolizes sex. Sex is literally everywhere. Our commercials are filled with half-naked women and men that appeal to the lust of our eyes. Sex has become a big money bracket. In our culture, "sex sells."

God gives us clear instruction not to lust after anyone sexually.

Remember Jesus said, "So a man thinks in his heart, so is he."

In Matthew 5:28 Jesus also said whoever looks at a woman (and this can be vice versa) to lust after her has already committed adultery for her in his heart. This is heavy because adultery alludes to marriage. If a husband looks at another woman in a sexual way, he has already broken his vows in his heart. If he doesn't take those thoughts captive it's just a matter of time before those thoughts and images enter his heart and chart out a course of adultery. Continuing in verse 29 He goes on to say that if your right eye makes you stumble, tear it out and throw it from you; for it is better to lose one of the parts of your body then your whole body be thrown into hell.

Now I don't believe Jesus was saying to literally pluck your eye out. He was saying that the things make us sin can be so a part of our lives that we feel like it is part of our own bodies. In other words, it's hard to stop looking at TV shows that have great story lines but also have explicit sex scenes. It almost makes you mad. Why did they have to mess up a good story with that mess? It makes us have to stop and make tough decisions about what to "pluck" out of our lives.

Job in the Bible made that decision. He tells us in Job 31 that he made a "covenant with his eyes."

He asks this question, "Why then should I look upon a maid?"

Job makes a promise with himself that he will not "gaze" or continuously think on the beauty of a young woman because he will probably end up thinking sexually about her in his heart and acting out his lust.

Remember, what's in your heart will come out.

It's the same with the ears. The Bible says in 2 Corinthians 10:5 that we are to "cast down" imaginations and "take captive" any thoughts that try to exalt itself against the knowledge of God.

We are to guard our hearts' affections. The "issues" of our heart. We don't want our affections to form into lusts. God wants to attach ourselves to Him and the things that come from him. Lust causes us to desire the things that Satan offers. Satan is a con artist. He loves to take the good God creates and warp it into something that will satisfy our sinful nature. Don't let him do that! Guard what you are hearing and what you are watching!

Your eyes and ears are the front doors to your heart. What things should be on *your* security list?

What kinds of movies, music, social media, TV, friends, family, magazines, blogs, etc. should be on your security list, and how do you know who and what should have access to the doors of your heart?

God has an answer for that as well. He tells us what to think on and what to look upon.

> Philippians 4:8-9
> Finally, brethren, whatever is true, whatever is honorable, whatever is right, whatever is pure, whatever is lovely, whatever is of good repute, if there is any excellence and if anything worthy of praise, dwell on these things. The things you have learned and received and heard and seen in me, practice these things, and the God of peace will be with you.

TAKE IT TO HEART

Let's do the Philippians 4:8 test. This will aid in making your own *security list*.

Here is how it works…

First answer these questions:

1. What is your favorite TV show?

2. Who is your favorite singer or band?

3. What is your favorite trend or social media pastime?

4. What is your favorite genre of book, magazine, or blog?

5. Who are your closest friends?

Use the chart below to characterize each answer by tallying synonyms and antonyms for each of your favorite things. In order for them to be placed on your security list, they need to have more synonyms than antonyms.

TRUE		NOBLE		PURE		LOVELY		ADMIRABLE	
Synonyms	Antonyms	Synonyms	Antonyms	Synonyms	Antonyms	Synonyms	Antonyms	Synonyms	Antonyms
Correct	Wrong	Dignified	Unlovely	Moral	Dirty	Beauty	Unkind	Great	Despicable
Honest	Flawed	Excellent	Undignified	Modest	Immodest	Enjoyable	Unpleasant	Excellent	Bad
Accurate	Evil	Queenly	Indecent	Good	Dark	Pleasant	Disagreeable	Praise-Worthy	Unworthy

My favorite TV show is_____

Synonyms (#   )   Antonyms (#   )   Security List (yes or no)

My favorite music/song is _____

Synonyms (#   )   Antonyms (#   )   Security List (yes or no)

My favorite book/magazine is _____

Synonyms (#   )   Antonyms (#   )   Security List (yes or no)

My favorite trend is _____

Synonyms (#   )   Antonyms (#   )   Security List (yes or no)

How many good qualities (synonyms) did your favorite things have? How many bad qualities (antonyms)?

_____

What things do you need to "take captive"?

_____

_____

Discuss and pray about this with someone. Ask a brother or sister in Christ to help keep you accountable with the things you have decided need to go.

It is extremely important to guard our thought life. One of the major ways we can do that is to guard our eyes and ears from ungodly and evil things.

Guarding the entrance to your heart by watching what you see and hear is so important that I thought I'd give you a few more daily ways to be mindful.

- ♥ Start your day by spending time with Jesus. Be sure to ask the Holy Spirit to help you guard your eyes and ears throughout the day.

- ♥ If a filthy commercial comes on while you are watching TV turn the channel until it's finished. If you have a DVR, you can record shows so that you can just fast forward through the commercials.

- ♥ Look at movie reviews prior to going to the movie theatre. Avoid movies that have sexual content, vulgar language or extreme violence.

- ♥ Put more music on your device that gives God praise. Music that uplifts Jesus and is filled with the Word of God will definitely have all those synonyms on that chart and more!

- ♥ Public places like the grocery store, the bowling alley, and the salon have all kinds of music playing that isn't good for your spirit. If you are at the salon, take some Christian music with you and put it in while you are sitting there.

After you leave the grocery store or the bowling alley ask the Lord to purify your heart from all the junk you were subconsciously listening to, and immediately play Christian music or listen to your Bible app.

♥ Remove yourself from gossip or unhealthy conversations.

So what and who will you give access to enter through your ears and eyes? Who or what will you allow on your security list?

My Security List

_____

_____

_____

_____

_____

_____

_____

_____

Detection System

When we arrive at the detention home and the control room has identified us on the security list; we must go through a metal detector and lock down anything that we have on our persons that could be a potential harm. Things like keys, cell phones, watches, and wallets are all things that we need in our lives, but not only are they not needed in the facility; they can be used by the detainees for harmful purposes or breakouts.

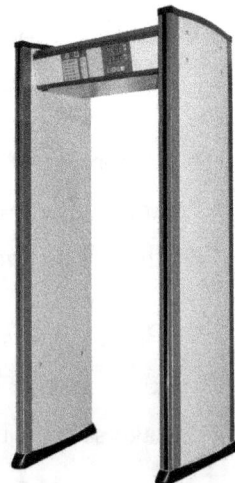

How does this relate to guarding the affections of our hearts?

Well, some information we receive is needed for our lives, but it can be harmful if we place our affections on some of that information.

For example, when I was in the sixth grade I was introduced to Darwinism. The information that man came from monkeys was information I needed to know to pass my tests, but I could not afford to let myself let that information sink into my heart—my belief system. Things like learning about different religions and hearing other people's thoughts about God, Jesus, and the purpose of life were always around me, but I had to learn to separate opinion from fact. Remember John 14:6? Jesus said, "I am the _____, the _____, and the _____.

It's important that we remember that God is Truth, and He gives us the Bible so that we can determine what truth is.

We have to be very careful not to meditate on untruths so intensely that they get past our detection and enter into our hearts and become who we are. Remember, "You are what you think."

Consider the Bible to be your metal detector. 2 Timothy 3:16 says, "All Scripture is inspired by God and profitable for teaching, for *reproof*, for *correction*, for *training* in *righteousness…*"

Hebrews 4:12 states the Word of God is *living and active and sharper than any two-edged sword, and piercing as far as the division of soul and spirit, of both joints and marrow, and able to judge the thoughts and intentions of the heart.*

Let's recap. When you read the Bible or hear the Word of God preached it enters your eye and ear entrance doors and it detects these things…

- ♥ what's in your soul and your spirit

- ♥ the thoughts of your heart

- ♥ the intentions of your heart

The Word of God not only detects but it corrects. Okay. Say that three times fast!

Not only detects but corrects

Not only detects but corrects

Not only detects but corrects

It is sharper than any two-edged sword. I always wondered what the difference between one and two edges was.

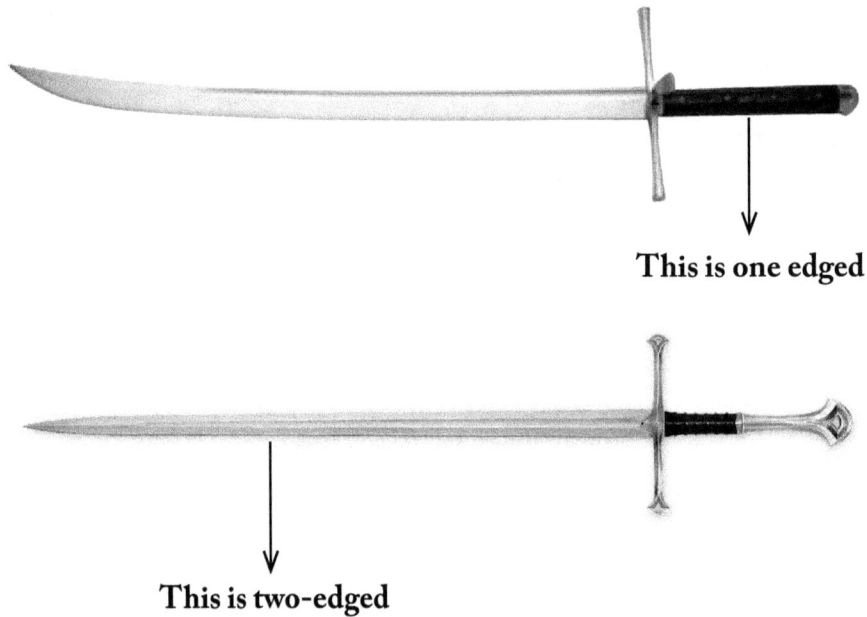

This is one edged

This is two-edged

If you have just one edge you can only cut one way. It means the message only reaches to your natural response but not your spiritual response. It would mean that maybe your thoughts were judged and not your intentions.

Our opinions and ideals are a lot like a one-edged sword. We fight only one opponent at a time without seeing the enemy as a whole. We judge people's appearances and we don't look at the character of a person. We look at the sin a person is in without considering why they have fallen into the enemy's trap. We ignore God when

He asks us to remember we don't fight against flesh and blood but evil (Ephesians 6:12). We often see our perspectives as truth, not realizing that they are mostly formed by our environments and exposures. We are ignorant of so many other sides. The Word of God is not like that. God explained to the prophet Samuel that man looks at the appearance of a person, but He judges the heart.

God's Word is even SHARPER than a sword with two edges. It divides the soul and spirit perfectly. Somehow divides it between how you respond naturally and how you respond spiritually. God's truth addresses not only what you think about something but *why* you think that way.

TAKE IT TO HEART

What kinds of messages get past your ears and eyes that you know does not agree with the Word of God?

_____

_____

_____

These messages can be helpful to past tests, or understand different cultures or beliefs, or even to help you in your career, but they are not rooted in the truth of the Word of God.

John 14:6, "I [Jesus] am the way, the truth, and the life. No one comes to the Father but through me."

The Word of God not only detects, but it corrects. This is also part of the Detection system that I call "locker security."

Once God's Word detects wrongful perspectives, intentions, beliefs, or thoughts it corrects, reproves, and trains you in the right way. It locks up what you don't need, and helps you understand why you don't need it.

In the Detention Center, we constantly need the lockers at our disposal to put away everything that would potentially be an obstacle and even dangerous for the students we are there to serve. When I first went in as a volunteer I didn't understand why I had to lock up my cell phone and keys before I went in. It was pretty frustrating until I realized that the written bylaws of the facility were there to protect the kids and the volunteers. I had to rely and trust the word of the facility and that's similar to how we simply trust God's Word. He knows what can cause us harm even when it seems safe to us. God's Word detects the harmful things in our hearts and gives us explanations on why they are harmful.

I had great parents. I grew up getting spankings, but they were few and far between. You know why? Because Mom and Dad just didn't tell me *not* to do something without telling me the consequences that would follow.

I understood you put on deodorant because if you don't, you will run all your friends away when you play kick ball. I understood that if you don't eat your vegetables you will end up with a weak body that won't be able to go on summer vacation with the rest of the family. Get the picture?

On a more serious note, God's Word is like that. Forgive so that you will be forgiven. Honor your mother and your father so you will have a long life. Believe in Jesus so that you won't spend eternity in a hell that was designed for demonic forces. Don't have sex out of marriage because your body is the temple of God, and fornication is a sin against your own body. It causes damage externally and internally. God is a loving father who desires that we are aware of what to do and why. The Bible says that he disciplines us or corrects us out of His love. 1 John tells us that God is love, so He has a perfect knowledge of what is best for us.

It is important to know God's Word so that we can detect lies from the enemy. If God's Word is not in us then how can it detect falsehood? How can God's Word be in you if you don't study it and listen to it preached?

King David understood this when he said "thy word have I hidden in my heart that I might not sin against you."

In Ephesians we are told to take captive thoughts that try to exalt themselves against the knowledge of God.

How are you doing with knowing God's Word? Do you read it every day? Do you attend a group that helps you to study it? Can you divide between lies and truth using the Word of God?

Do you feel you have allowed too many of the devil's lies to enter into your heart?

It's not too late to run and get your Bible and look up the truth that will detect lies, correct, and train you in what is right.

Answer these questions?

1. Do you believe God exists? If so, why?

2. Do you believe Jesus died for your sins? If so, why and how do you know that's true?

3. Do you believe as long as you are saved it's okay to do what you want?

4. Do you think sex outside of marriage is okay as long as you love the person?

5. It's okay to listen and watch anything you want. It does not affect you. True or False

6. Truth is anything you choose to believe. True or False

Now read these verses and see if there is any falsehood to what you believe.

1. Romans 1:12; Hebrews 11:6; Psalm 14:1; Genesis 1:27; Revelations 4:11

2. 1 Peter 3:18; 1 Corinthians 15:3-4; Hebrews 9:28; John 3:16; Hebrews 10:12-14

3. John 3:3; 2 Corinthians 5:17; John 16:8; Romans 6:1-2; 1 Corinthians 10:31

4. 1 Corinthians 6:18-20; Hebrews 13:4; Revelation 21:8; 1 Corinthians 6:9-10

5. Mark 4:24; Matthew 13:16; Matthew 5:28; Matthew 6:22-23

6. John 14:6; Deuteronomy 18:20-22; 2 Peter 1:21; John 14:17, Romans 12:1-2

When Jesus left he didn't leave us "orphans." He left us the Holy Spirit and His job is to lead us into all truth. The Holy Spirit does not say anything to us that is against the Bible or contradict the Bible.

Pray and ask the Holy Spirit to show you the thoughts that are not rooted in the truth of God's Word. Find scriptures that teach you what is right about the falsehood you've received and repent, change your mind about it and let God's truth transform your beliefs (Romans 12:1-2).

The Lobby

Most wouldn't consider a lobby part of a security plan, but it is very vital to ensure that there are no breaches in security or there are no impostors.

The lobby also is a point of grace. many times I have entered through the doors because I was on the security list. I was able to bypass the detectors and the lockers and didn't realize my keys were in my pocket. When I'm sitting in the lobby waiting for a certain officer to escort me back to the heart of the facility, I usually have time to realize I have something on me that needs to go back and be locked away. I realize I have something that needs to be divided from my persons. I need my keys to operate in the natural, but I don't need my keys to operate in the spiritual when I'm ministering to the kids in the facility.

The lobby is also important because there are guards sitting in the offices that can give you more information about your purpose for being there. There is usually one specific officer called to meet us at this point and make sure we understand our rights and a form that asks us to choose to deny ourselves and follow the facilities protocol. The lobby is a waiting place for the informant—a reflective place. It's the general area. In the lobby you have a lot of company. There are other visitors, new detainees are coming through, guards and officers, and other officials. There is also a lot of conversation and commotion in the lobby.

As we are guarding our hearts it is important to realize that we are in a RELA-TIONSHIP with Jesus. He LIVES in our hearts and we are in His. The greatest affection we have as a child of God is for Jesus, but as in any relationship, there are distractions and obligations. It's easy to get caught up in the "cares" of this world. A lot of things and people make it to our "lobbies" but they should be assessed to make sure they do not take the number-one seat of our affection. Only Jesus should have that seat.

Here are some things that make it through the security system, and are now waiting in the lobby:

1. Family

2. Friends

3. Spouse

4. Education

5. Career

6. Hobbies

7. Recreation

8. Physical Fitness

9. Intellect

These things can be good for our lives and even necessary. For the most part, there is no reason to separate them from our lives or our thoughts. They hold no poison or metals of destruction and we have great affection for them, but as we go deeper into the center of our hearts we find that some of these things must fill out a waiver form while they are in the lobby. Before these things enter deep into our hearts they must be aware that they cannot take first place. They can't sit on the seat of our primary affection. They have to submit to the terms of the facility and a heart that follows God has the rule that only God is the first love of the heart.

A beautiful example of this is when Jesus was preaching and his disciples informed Him that His mother and siblings were waiting to speak with him. Jesus didn't stop preaching and jump up to see what they wanted. Instead, he explained that those who did the will of his Father were his mother and his brothers (Matthew 12:46-48).

I know how this feels. Many times I felt second fiddle to the detention home ministry. At times I felt my parents loved other children more than me. It wasn't easy, but because they loved God first and obeyed him fully I was greatly affected and God began to move on my heart. I ended up experiencing Christ through the ministry and serving the children I was once jealous of. So you see, it wasn't that Jesus didn't love his mother and brothers. Jesus prioritized the will of the Father, because God was his first love. It was because Jesus was fully obedient to the Father that his mother and brothers had the opportunity to be made right with God and inherit eternal life. When we love God and prioritize His will over our own we find our other relationships are better off. The people in our lives can have a front-row seat to the glory of God when we surrender to His work in our hearts.

Transitional Holding Area
(Secret Chamber; Importance of Prayer)

We have already mentioned this before but each detention facility is different. In the one we are using there is a space between the lobby and the pod area. This room is very small and it has locked doors all the way around with a camera in the corner. I call this space the transitional holding area.

This space is your transit to your destination, but there is a waiting period to make sure all is well before you move forward. When I first went into the facility this space was the most intimidating because it was so confining and the security camera was so noticeable; it was like it was looking right through you. Everyone gets so quiet in this area. Another part of this space is the speakers that connect to the control room. While you are waiting, often you will hear the officer in the control room give you final instructions and reminders before you enter into the core of the facility. It's your last chance to check your pockets. Remember, anything you may need, or even to confirm your commitment. After this you're escorted to the pods where the treasure is kept. Does this transitional holding area remind you of any part of your relationship with Christ? What words or concepts stood out to you?

How about "waiting," "looking right through you," "quiet," "hear," "instructions," or "confirm your commitment"?

_____   _____   _____

Unlike the lobby, where there can be a lot of outside influence, distraction, and noise; this room is quiet and places you in an environment where the Word of God causes you to really confirm your commitment to Christ. Are you truly a follower? I don't just mean do you believe in Jesus and know stuff about Him, but have you really denied yourself, signed the waiver of the cross, and decided to follow Christ come what may? This is a place where you can change your mind?

Look in your pockets. Do you still have that picture or the souvenir from your sinful life? Are you still holding on to love letters from your past lust, your idol, or your selfish ambition?

This is your time to bask in the presence of God. Allow God to look right through your heart. God sees what's in your heart, but there is something about permitting Him to reveal your motives. Why do you have the friends you have? Why do you hold so dearly to things that may be harmful? Why do you listen to that music and idolize that celebrity? Why do you hate your dad? Why are you angry at the world? Why do you want to go to college? These are just some examples of questions you could ask yourself and God to help you with the answers. Use the space below to write out your motives. Feel free to use some of the above questions to help you get started.

_____

_____

_____

_____

_____

_____

_____

_____

_____

_____

Why do you have the friends you have? Why do you hold so dearly to things that may be harmful? Why do you listen to that music and idolize that celebrity? Why do you hate your dad? Why are you angry at the world? Why do you want to go to college?

Jesus doesn't just care about what we do. He also deeply cares about why we do them. (Proverbs 16:2, Jeremiah 17:10)

Jesus also deeply cares about where our affections lie. He cares about who and what has our hearts and WHY?

Another word for this area is your "secret chamber." When Jesus talked about praying He explained you shouldn't make a show of it (Matthew 6:6). He said it's an intimate time. You should go into your closet, shut the door behind you, and pray to your Father and the Father who sees in secret will reward you openly.

When Agape Ambassadors are in this area and leave freedom to enter into captivity it is very common for many of us to reflect on our motives. As I hear those steel doors shut all around me I often ask myself and God, "why am I doing this?"

This is a place where Jesus's statement magnifies itself in my reality.

Am I willing to deny myself, take up my cross, and follow Jesus; even if it is in a prison to share him with teenagers that society may have given up on?

Am I doing this to make myself feel good about myself or am I doing this for God's glory?

Am I doing this, or anything else for self to be satisfied or for God to be pleased?

This is where our hearts are tested and tried. That's why I call it a transition, because your heart is moving from one state to another. This is the place where you don't just know the Bible, but you encounter the Spirit of Truth. This is the place where you see Jesus, maybe not literally or in the flesh, although God can reveal himself as He pleases, whether that be visions or dreams; but it is the place where you transition from your will to God's will.

What do I mean? Jesus also taught this about prayer in Matthew. When you pray you should pray to God, "your kingdom come, your will be done, on earth as it is in heaven."

Take a look at this:

Prayer IS	Prayer is NOT
Humbly coming to God realizing He is in Heaven; the ruler of heaven and earth.	A Christmas list to Santa
Realizing that God knows all and you don't.	All about you and what you want
Being willing to accept God's decisions even if you don't understand.	Trying to change God's mind to accommodate what you think is best
Trusting God's character to want what He wants no matter what and being willing to wait, believe, and obey.	Demanding God to agree with your desires
Absolutely vital to your growth as a Christian. It is your connection to your Father in Heaven. The Bible tells us that we should always pray and pray without ceasing.	A pastime or just a hobby
The Bible tells us that the prayers of the righteous accomplish much. It takes discipline and, there's power in prayer. My grandfather has been a pastor and evangelist for years and he always says, "when the church prays, God moves." Prayer moves God to act on our behalf. Read the accounts of Daniel, Esther, David, Elijah, the disciples, Paul, JESUS…. Check out the powerful results of prayer in and through their lives. The disciples saw such powerful results, and because of Jesus' prayer life they were moved to ask him to teach them. Men who had been taught to pray all their lives, and literally were taught prayers for every occasion were asking Jesus to TEACH them how to pray. They saw something different in the prayers Jesus prayed.	For the weak Used to impress people of how 'religious' or 'righteous' you are Something that should be neglected or taken lightly. It's important to remember who you are praying to and God should always be reverenced and respected even though He delights in hearing from you

Where's your secret closet? Where is the place where you take your heart to God and allow him to search it, test it, reveal it, and change it?

TAKE IT TO HEART

Design your own secret chamber. You can answer these questions and feel free to add your own. This is just to get you started. You can also feel free to put the things you would like to talk to God about. You can also use illustrations in your design.

Your secret chamber can accommodate where you are. You may be in a detention facility. Your prayer chamber can be your cell. You may be at home, and you could use your bedroom or another room in the house. You can even use a real closet. I personally love my back porch. Maybe you are an outdoor person, and there is a spot in the yard that you go to spend time in prayer. Jesus prayed a lot outside! He loved mountains and gardens. Take time to pick a place and set intentional times where you can meet with God.

Where is your secret chamber?	What are the things you will bring with you in this place of prayer?
What makes the place a private place for you and God?	What times will you set to meet God here?

There are just a few more things about this special place I'd like to elaborate on. It's a place of maturity, intimacy, and stillness.

A Place of Maturity (Hebrews 11, 1 Corinthians 14:20, Romans 12:1-2)

♥ This is where you trust God. The Bible tells us that the righteous walks by faith and not by sight and that takes maturity. Faith comes by hearing the Word of God over and over and over again. The more you hear it the more you believe God, and the more you trust Him to reveal even the secret sins of your heart that no one knows anything about. It takes real maturity to say, "I'm sorry." When you spend time with Jesus, let Him know that you are sorry, and you want to stop doing the things you know hurt HIS heart.

♥ This is where you are grown in Christ to ask Him the tough questions about yourself? Are you mature enough to ask God if He really is pleased with the decisions you've been making? Are you mature enough to ask Him? Are you really ready for what you've been praying for? How about asking yourself do you really love the Lord with all your heart, soul, mind, and strength? Here's a tough one: have you really received forgiveness for all your sins and have you forgiven that person that really did you wrong?

Jehovah Jireh- The Lord my provider	Jehovah Roi- The Lord who sees	Adonai- Lord, Master
Jehovah Nissi- The Lord my banner	Jehovah Shalom-God of peace	Jehovah Rapha-The Lord who heals

A Place of Intimacy (Jeremiah 29:11, 1 John 1:9, John 15:4-6, Philippians 4:6)

God trusts you with His plans.

♥ Remember how God talked to Abraham about destroying Sodom and Gomorrah before he did it? If not, check out Genesis 18:16-33.

♥ God begins "surgery" with His Word and the Spirit of Truth begins to roll up the shades so you can see what God sees

♥ God chastises those He loves and begins to convict you about where you need to stop something or He compels you to start something.

♥ You breathe in His goodness and breathe out your anxieties.

♥ You speak His Word back to Him and you love on Him with your worship.

♥ Let Him heal your heart. Forgive those who have wronged you and forgive yourself. Let God mend your broken heart.

A Place of Stillness (Psalm 46:10, Psalm 18:3, Romans 10:13)

♥ Practice being still; just take a deep breath and focus all your thoughts on Jesus. Try calling out some of his names. I have given you a few names of God with scripture that you can think on

♥ Pray and talk with God but remember this is a place where your words become few. Say what is necessary, but then, "Be still and know that God is God."

♥ Take time to just listen. Jesus said in John 10 that He is the good shepherd and His sheep hear His voice and a stranger they will not follow. If you know the Word of God and study your Bible, you can rightly discern if the still small voice you may hear is Jesus. Now, you may not hear anything. I don't make a habit of putting God in a box. He is God and I will not dare place a formula on how He chooses to work, speak, or reveal; but I can tell you that He will not speak anything that is against the Bible, and He will not say anything that opposes the fact that Jesus is the God in flesh.

♥ The Bible instructs us to test every spirit because, remember, Satan is out there speaking too. He knows the Bible probably better than most of us, and he loves to use it and mix it with his lies and wants to lead us to completely compromise the course God wants to keep us on. Watch out! Satan is a thief and he desires to steal the Word of God from our hearts so we don't believe and we don't act on right beliefs. He wants to steal this quiet time because he knows it is so powerful. He knows that when you pray, God changes you and you are able to change things because God receives your prayers and delights to answer them! It is Satan's priority to cause you to be so busy and distracted—even by good things—that you don't have time to meet God in your secret place. Don't let him do that!

♥ Commit to your time where you secretly meet with God. Place on hold everything and everyone that causes you to keep moving and inhibits you from being still in God's presence

♥ Close your eyes, relax, and rest in the arms of Jesus. Let Him whisper you the truths of His Word and to encourage your heart that He is faithful, good, reliable, trustworthy, and he loves you like CRAZY!!!!

♥ There is no agenda in this secret place, there is no to-do list behind your back; it's just you and your heavenly DADDY! Be still and just know that your heavenly Daddy is the Almighty God! He has lavished His love on you, sacrificed His only Son for you, and calls you His son and His daughter.

The Pods

For our purposes, the pods represent where the treasure safely resides. In the facility, we see the pods as storehouses with souls ready to hear the Gospel of Christ and be transformed by the message of God's grace through Jesus. The pods are where the ministry spends most of its time while we are at the facility. It's the core and the center of our attention. The pods are the area of our destination. It is the reason why we go through all the security measures. The pods hold the treasure of identity and change in the world.

The pods represent our heart, the kids represent our affections, and in our hearts', also lie our confession of faith in Jesus Christ. Many things dwell in our hearts, but we have been zoning in on our affections for our first love.

Within our confession of faith in Jesus lies an affection to be just like Him. That affection, if closely secured, will take our lives on a course that results in the most ultimate gratification on this earth, but also for all eternity. Through Jesus, our hearts are able to enter into a love relationship with God that can last forever. Sin separates, but the cross connects, and it's through Jesus our hearts can beat for the Creator who designed them. The Blood of Jesus washes our sins white as snow and puts us on good terms with God. We are not good in God's sight because we just got it going on. No. No. NO. "It is by grace that we are saved, not by works lest any man should boast" (Ephesians 2:8)

Many things in our lives compete for our attention. In my life, some of these things are good and some are not good at all. Some good things that grab after my affection are family and friends, but in the world things like sex, money, and selfish gain try to grab at my attention. Every day I must be careful of what my eyes see and what my ears hear. Every day it's important to read, study, and say God's Word. It's also important to daily ask God to forgive me for my mistakes and empower me to walk in right paths with Him; not go my own way. Every day I have to sit still in His presence and focus my thoughts on Him. If I don't spend time reading my Bible and being still before God, my heart drowns in all the things the world wants me to pay attention to. I will get caught up in fear because of bad news, and I will get caught up in worrying about how to take care of myself and my family, thus, forgetting that God is my life and my keeper. He takes care of me, and there is safety in Jesus.

Remember at the beginning of the book we talked about how Proverbs 4:23 explained that we are to guard our hearts because out of it flows the issues of life. Another way to think of it is our lives are mapped out by what's in our hearts? Well, when your ultimate heart affection is for Jesus He infuses you with His desires and gives you the affections you need to have in order to have the abundant life He came to give you. Yes, we make mistakes and even get off course. We even try to take detours and shortcuts, but when Christ is our center affection and we put Him back on the throne of our hearts, He will always put us on track.

When I was in college the ultimate affection of my heart was me. I was sitting on the throne of my soul. I was so selfish! I wanted my way all the time, and I didn't care who I hurt. I thought for sure I knew what was best for me, and I wanted God's promises for my life, but not the process. In other words, I just wanted the "good stuff" from God that made me feel good, not understanding that God's priority was not my feelings. I wanted to be influential. I wanted to share Jesus with others, and I did on many occasions, but I was having a hard time letting God have all of me. I wanted to keep some control. I wanted to teach kids, but I wanted to make money. I wanted to write and sing, but I wanted to be popular. Have you ever felt like that? You want good things in life, but you want them for your agenda not God's? I cared more about pleasing myself and fulfilling my friends' agendas than I did about God's plan for me. I had terrible self-esteem and thought my value was based on how much I was needed by others. My motivation for helping people rested on feeling important, not realizing how valuable I was already. This self-absorption was self-worship, and it became such a destructive affection in my heart that my life was going down a course of loneliness, lust, backbiting, and rebellion. I had accumulated so much bitterness, unforgiveness, guilt, distrust, and deceit, that I didn't even know if God really loved me or if He would ever forgive me, but thanks be to God He did! How do I know He did? I began to seek after God. I couldn't get enough of meeting with God in secret and reading His Word. I put 1 John 1:9 to memory and trusted God that He wouldn't lie. I started to believe this particular promise was for me. Guess what? This promise is for you! Take a look at this scripture and write it down with your name included in it. That's right. Make is personal.

_____

_____

_____

Jesus helped me step off the throne of my heart. Have you ever played the trust game? My dad used to play it with my brother and me when we were kids. We turned our backs to Dad and he would say, "Fall back!"

We would fall completely back and completely trust him to catch us. That is how he taught us what trusting God feels like. Well, I had forgotten how to just fall back and trust God to catch me. I wanted control in everything, not realizing I had very little control over anything. Think about it. How much control do you really have? Make a list.

Things I have COMPLETE control over	Things I have NO control over

If you're honest, you see that there is very little we have complete control over. Some leave it to chance or luck, but will you choose to trust a God that is intentional about everything and takes such care of your life? He takes more care over your life and your heart than you do. Maybe you're saying, "I don't know, Jessica. I just don't think I can just fall back on God. I don't think I can completely trust Him with providing for my family. I don't think He can get me out of this addiction or this abusive relationship. How can I just trust him? I am afraid God will disappoint me like so many others have."

I understand your fears and concerns. No, I really do. I have thought the same things at many times in my life. Can I share something with you? It is safer to trust a God who sees all and can do all things than to trust ourselves. We don't know everything. We can't see into tomorrow much less way down the road, but God can. That's why Proverbs 3:5-6 tells us not to rely on our understanding, but trust in the Lord with all our hearts and acknowledge Him. Guess what He will do? He will direct us. He will put us on right paths. Before you can acknowledge God, you have to acknowledge the fact that He is God and you are not. You are not in control. I am not in control. Sure, we are able to work, live, function, impact lives, make goals— all of that is good to do—but we can do nothing without God. He even gives us the breath we breathe. It's in Christ that we live, move, and have our very being (Acts 17:28).

I learned to place the crown of my trust on Christ's head right with his crown of LORD of lords. I began to trust God more and more and eventually I put the robe of my most precious cares around his shoulders. If he bore the sins of the world on his shoulders he can surely handle my little worries no matter how big they may seem to me. I had to and you must learn to trust him with EVERYTHING. He's already KING of KINGS and LORD of LORDS, but it is beneficial for you to crown him Lord of YOUR heart, soul, and mind. I learned, as you will, that all my other desires and affections needed to branch out from the root of my affection for Jesus.

FAMILY   WORTH   INFLUENCE   FRIENDS

FINANCES   EDUCATION   PARENTS   AFRAID TO MAKE MISTAKES

TAKE IT TO HEART

Name the crowns and robes with the areas of your life that you feel you try to govern. Feel free to cross out my examples if they don't relate to you. After identifying these areas, ask the Holy Spirit to help you release these things and place them under Christ's authority. On this page, give your "crowns" and "robes" to Jesus by writing them around His throne. His hands are open, waiting for you to surrender to Him, every part of your heart.

Art by Travis Fernatt

The Control Room

Eye of the Operation

Guarding your heart may seem like an impossible task.

Would you agree that your heart can be a little overwhelming at times? I mean, let's face it. It's a huge task to manage.

There's watching what you watch and hear. There's being mindful of entertaining thoughts that like to run toward the world instead of God, and let's not forget all those affections and desires that can creep up to the throne of our hearts and try to boot Jesus off.

It's A LOT!

Take heart! No pun intended ☺

You are not alone in this security system. In this chapter I want you to understand that God is in control. He sees and He is the Almighty God. When we walk out of the transitional holding area, we see a big booth surrounded by glass, and there are usually many computers in there with someone manning the booth. The computers show everything that is going on in the facility. The person behind the computers is not only responsible for keeping an eye on the detainees but also all the surrounding areas that are connected to the pods. This includes everything from the parking lot to the cafeteria. It wouldn't be much of a security system if there were only cameras in the pods would it? No. Someone has to stay on post and watch everything that's going on.

There is someone who is standing watch over us all the time. Not only our hearts but everything about us. There is nothing about us that misses His eye. He is what I'd like to call the "eye of the operation."

I bet you already guessed who this is. You're right if you said God. God is in control. God's throne is a place of authority over the heavens and the earth. All things are under His jurisdiction.

There is no border you can cross that is out of God's power, authority, wisdom, and judgment. He is All-Seeing, Almighty, All-powerful, All-knowing, All-sufficient, and All-wise. The Bible says that He neither slumbers nor sleeps (Psalm 121:4) and He never gets tired or weary (Isaiah 40:28). That means God NEVER falls asleep on the job.

Let's take a look at Psalms 139. Highlight or circle parts in this Psalm that indicate God knows you, sees you, created you, and cares for you.

Psalm 139 English Standard Version (ESV)

¹O Lord, you have searched me and known me!
²You know when I sit down and when I rise up;
 you discern my thoughts from afar.
³You search out my path and my lying down
 and are acquainted with all my ways.
⁴Even before a word is on my tongue,
 behold, O Lord, you know it altogether.
⁵You hem me in, behind and before,
 and lay your hand upon me.
⁶Such knowledge is too wonderful for me;
 it is high; I cannot attain it.
⁷Where shall I go from your Spirit?
 Or where shall I flee from your presence?
⁸If I ascend to heaven, you are there!
 If I make my bed in Sheol, you are there!

⁹If I take the wings of the morning
  and dwell in the uttermost parts of the sea,
¹⁰even there your hand shall lead me,
  and your right hand shall hold me.

¹¹If I say, "Surely the darkness shall cover me,
  and the light about me be night,"
¹²even the darkness is not dark to you;
  the night is bright as the day,
  for darkness is as light with you.
¹³For you formed my inward parts;
  you knitted me together in my mother's womb.
¹⁴I praise you, for I am fearfully and wonderfully made.
  Wonderful are your works;
  my soul knows it very well.
¹⁵My frame was not hidden from you,
  when I was being made in secret,
  intricately woven in the depths of the earth.
¹⁶Your eyes saw my unformed substance;
  in your book were written, every one of them,
  the days that were formed for me,
  when as yet there was none of them.
¹⁷How precious to me are your thoughts, O God!
  How vast is the sum of them!
¹⁸If I would count them, they are more than the sand.
  I awake, and I am still with you.
¹⁹Oh that you would slay the wicked, O God!
  O men of blood, depart from me!
²⁰They speak against you with malicious intent;
  your enemies take your name in vain.
²¹Do I not hate those who hate you, O Lord?
  And do I not loathe those who rise up against you?

²²I hate them with complete hatred;
  I count them my enemies.
²³Search me, O God, and know my heart!
  Try me and know my thoughts!
²⁴And see if there be any grievous way in me,
  and lead me in the way everlasting.

In the space below, write or draw things in your life that you believe God sees and cares deeply about.

_____

_____

_____

_____

_____

_____

God who Sees

(El Roi)

Before we move on, I want to stop and address a woman in the Bible who realized that God sees everything and He really does care.

Turn your Bibles to Genesis 16. Read the whole chapter and answer these questions.

Who was Hagar?

_____

_____

_____

Why did Hagar run away?

_____

_____

_____

Who did Hagar meet as she was fleeing?

_____

_____

_____

What was the message from this visitor?

_____

_____

_____

What was Hagar's response?

_____

_____

_____

What name did Hagar give to God?

_____

Have you ever tried to run away from a situation? Have you ever been like Hagar where your heart just couldn't face the trouble in your life? God sees you. He sees you right now as you read this workbook. Don't try to hide things that are in your heart. Don't try to run away from God or your responsibilities. Come clean. Share your heart with God and allow Him to impregnate you with hope. That hope is found in Jesus, the Son of God. God not only sees you, but He is ready to listen because He cares deeply for you.

What is your response to such a caring and all-seeing God?

_____

_____

_____

_____

_____

Almighty God

It's important to remember God not only sees everything, but He is able to do anything. Nothing is impossible for Him.

Why don't you try to memorize this verse?

Luke 1:37, "For nothing will be impossible with God."

God is not in the control room because He is nosy and just wants to have knowledge of what's going on. He does not distance Himself from what we are going through. As a matter of fact, God asked Jeremiah if He is a God near and not a God far off? (23:23). Remember Psalm 139? God's presence is everywhere. One of my favorite scriptures talks about God's presence with His people and His power in Numbers 11. Here the Israelites are tired of manna and they want meat to eat. They are throwing a temper tantrum, and Moses has had it up to his ears with their complaining. He has a very interesting talk with God and is so upset with his call to lead these people he asks God to kill him. The LORD makes him a promise he will give meat to all these millions of people. Moses is finding it hard to believe that God can provide meat for all of them. God says in verse 23, is the LORD's hand shortened? Now you shall see whether My Word will come true for you or not."

Some translations say, "is the LORD's arm too short?"

God is willing and more than able to perform His Word. The book of Numbers tells us that God is not like a man he should lie or change his mind. He will do what he says. All throughout the Bible from the Old Testament to the New Testament He promises a Savior who would rescue us from the strong grip of sin. God made good on His promise. There is physical proof and accounts of a man named Jesus who lived and died. There were eyewitness accounts of those who saw Him resurrected from the dead. We have some of those accounts in the Gospels. The validity of the Bible has proven true and no one has been able to discredit it over the hundreds of years it has been compiled to what we know today. Jesus told the people of His day that if they didn't believe He was the Son of God, to at least believe in the works that He did.

You can depend on God. He is trustworthy. There are times when I was like Moses, and I would ask God if what the Bible was saying really applied to me. Could and would God really give me strength to work and go to college, wisdom to make good decisions, and health at a time when my body was in pain? God never let me down, and He has never failed me or disappointed me. I can look back on all my hard times and see how it was God alone who put the right people in place, encouraged me, healed me, and led me on right paths. God has no weaknesses, limitations or needs. He says that even if he *was* hungry he wouldn't tell you; why? Because the Earth and everything in it belongs to Him (Psalm 50:12). His arm is not too short to care for your heart, so place it in His hand.

God's Ultimate Security Plan

God always has a plan. I'll let you in on an exposed secret. His plan is always best. He's perfect in all of His ways. He is always right and He is never wrong. NEVER.

I talked to one young man in the detention home, and he had recently given his heart to Christ. He said one of his favorite scriptures was Proverbs 14:12, "There is a way *that seems* right to a man, but its end *is* the way of death."

When I asked him why he liked this verse he explained that before Christ he thought he was ALWAYS right, but it wasn't until he started reading the Bible that he found out that he didn't know as much as he thought. He explained that he had realized that his decisions were actually destroying his life. He saw that God's Word was what he needed to have a life that he could enjoy. In other words, God's Word was safety.

John 1:1-5 says,

"In the beginning was the Word, and the Word was with God, and the Word was God. *He* was in the beginning with God. All things were made through *Him,* and without *Him* was not anything made that was made. In *Him* was life, and the life was the light of men. The light shines in the darkness, and the darkness has not overcome it."

Notice something interesting this verse that talks about God's Word? The Word is called *Him.* Who is the Him? I'll give you one guess. Yep! Jesus Christ!

If you haven't gotten it already; that's the secret key to God's entire security plan, and that is the security plan that ensures true safety from sin and hell; it's Jesus Christ. It is only in Jesus that our hearts are safe. It is only in Jesus we will never perish in the lake of fire that is designed for Satan and his demons.

Jesus Christ is the whole reason our hearts are worth protecting. 2 Corinthians 5:17-21 says,

"Therefore, if anyone is in Christ, he is a new creation. The old has passed away; behold, the new has come. All this is from God, who through Christ reconciled us to himself and gave us the ministry of reconciliation; that is, in Christ, God was reconciling the world to himself, not counting their trespasses against them, and entrusting to us the message of reconciliation. Therefore, we are ambassadors for

Christ, God making his appeal through us. We implore you on behalf of Christ, be reconciled to God. For our sake he made him to be sin who knew no sin, so that in him we might become the righteousness of God."

Have you experienced that newness of life in Jesus Christ? We may not always feel saved, but rest assured that it is "by Grace you have been saved through faith, and this is not your own doing; it is a gift of God, not a result of works so that no one can boast" (Ephesians 2:8).

God not only created a plan to bring us back to Himself, but He Himself implemented the plan. He is not just sitting high and looking low, but He came low, made himself a little lower than the angels He created, He became sin for me and you to exchange our filthy rags of unrighteousness for His pure white linen of righteousness.

Jesus said, "What would it profit a man to gain this whole world and lose his own soul?" (Mark 8:36).

Understand that your soul is more valuable than the treasures of this whole world. Your heart is the most precious gift in the universe. It's your will, affection, passion, and obedience Jesus wants.

Also, I want to take the time to mention something very important. The story isn't over and God has one more promise that all believers in Christ are waiting on…. Christ's return and our glorified bodies. These bodies are affected by this fallen world and are decaying, our hearts are affected by this sinful world and need daily cleansing. With our best intentions we are still imperfect people, even though God's Spirit lives in us when we put our faith in Jesus; but there is an awesome promise found in John 14:3,

> "And if I go and prepare a place for you, I will come again
> and will take you to Myself, that where I am you may be also."

He's going to prepare an eternal place for us and He is coming back personally to take us to be with Him forever! Seriously?

Do you ever think about Jesus coming back for you? That's what I call a heart relationship. Christ's heart is for you, and He is coming to get you. Will He find your heart fully loving, trusting, and obeying Him when he returns?

TAKE IT TO HEART

What makes you feel secure?

_____

_____

_____

Who makes you feel insecure?

_____

_____

_____

What kind of environments make you feel uncomfortable or unsafe?

_____

_____

_____

How has sin in your life compromised your safety?

_____

_____

_____

What do you do to regain security that has been stolen?

_____

_____

Gaining or Regaining Security

What happens when the storms of life make our hearts shake with fear and feel anything but secure? How do we protect our heart's affection for Jesus alone when our needs and our hardships leave our hearts hungry for solutions and desperate for immediate salvation? It can be difficult to protect your love for Jesus in the hard times when it's so tempting to turn your heart toward the temporary security of people, systems, and material things. Let's take a close look at John chapter 6 and see how Jesus responds to us when our hearts need to be reminded that only He is our safety.

Read John 6:1-21

Answer the questions below.

John 6:1-6

Why were so many people following Jesus?

_____

_____

_____

Do you think these people were seeking security from Jesus? If so, what did you think they wanted security from?

_____

_____

As a huge number of people came towards Jesus, what question did He ask Philip?

_____

_____

Did He ask this question because He didn't know the answer? How do you know?

_____

_____

Verses 7-15

What was the only solution the disciples could come up with for this dilemma?

_____

_____

What did Jesus ask the people to do?

_____

_____

Why do you think Jesus wanted the people to sit down?

_____

_____

How many men were there?

_____

What did Jesus do with the food that was given him by the young boy?

_____

_____

Have you ever seen God multiply the little that you had and provide for not just you but people around you?

_____

_____

Did the huge crowd get the security they were expecting? Why or why not? (Matthew 14:21-23)

_____

_____

Have you ever seen Jesus do something in your life that was for your best but it wasn't necessarily what you prayed for? Share with a friend.

_____

_____

_____

_____

Verse 15: Why did Jesus leave and go up to the mountain? Why didn't He want the people to crown Him King when He _is_ King? (John 5:24, 41-47; Matthew 20:28)

_____

_____

Verses 16-21

Why were the disciples in a boat on the sea?

_____

_____

What happened while they were at sea?

_____

_____

Why were they afraid?

_____

_____

What security did they find in letting Jesus in the boat and what happened to their boat after they _willingly_ let Jesus in?

_____

_____

_____

In what area in your life do you need to willingly let Jesus in your situation? Do you need him to help you forgive? Do you feel unsafe in a relationship? Is there a storm in your mind? Have you given up on life?

_____

_____

_____

Even when we find our boats of life in the most ferocious winds and raging seas we can find security when we willingly allow Jesus in our boat. He makes our boats a place of safety no matter what is going on around us. You can think of your boat as your heart too. The storms of life can make our hearts shake with fear or rock with worry, but look past the storm and you'll find Jesus standing strong in the midst saying, "It is I; do not be afraid."

Receive him and watch him get you safely to land.

Who is Jesus? He is our Safety

God's ultimate battle plan to safeguard our hearts is centered on Jesus Christ. From the very beginning it was God's plan to send His only Son to save the world from sin. Adam and Eve's disobedience didn't catch God by surprise. He already was way ahead of Satan's plan to destroy the beautiful fellowship between God and His people. This chart is going to help us to see through God's Word how Jesus is our safety. He is God. He is the Son of God. He is fully man. All of who Jesus is can boggle our brain, but in Revelation 1:8, 17-18 He tells us exactly who He is. Read those verses and use the first cell to write down what Jesus says about himself.

Use the remainder of the chart to fill in the roles that Jesus has and how He is FOR us and AGAINST sin and Satan.

Revelations 1:8, 17-18	John 10:9 I Am the _____	John 10:14 I Am the _____ _____
Job 19:25 My _____ Lives!	Luke 2:11 A _____ is given!	Hebrews 3:1 _____
Isaiah 9:6 (a lot of names here!)	John 8:58 _____	John 1:29 _____
Hebrews 12:2 _____	Psalm 18:2 _____	Proverbs 21:31 _____ belongs to the LORD.

There are many people who rely on their spouses, their jobs, their intelligence, their beauty, their talents, and other things for their security. It's easy to put your trust in people and systems to uphold your security or that of your family. In times of desperation it is common to go to the quickest solution around us. It is easy to look at what we see and not trust in God whom we can't see. We often think that what we see is more efficient than what is invisible. The truth is that God asks us to have faith for a reason. Hebrews 11:1 tells us that faith is actually the substance of things hoped for and evidence of things we don't see. When we feel unsafe, unstable, or insecure the surest safety lies in our unshakeable faith and trust in Jesus Christ.

It is simply a choice. Life happens, true. There are going to be times our faith in Jesus will be shaken. Things will seem as though it will never work out or that God is too busy to handle our lives. Rest in God's promises. When God promises something it has to come to past because He cannot lie. Yes, Jesus told us our lives would be full of trials. Let's not ever think that we are exempt from hardship just because we are children of God. The difference between you and an unbeliever is that the Spirit of the one true living God lives in you, and He is greater than anything in this world (1 John 4:4). The truth is that Christ has given you every spiritual blessing that you need pertaining to this life (Ephesians 1:3). That's right! You have the Holy Spirit living in you and He comes with all kinds of fruit that can get you through whatever comes your way. Check out Galatians 5:22-23.

Apostle Paul is not talking about apples and oranges here. Read this scripture and write the fruit that he is talking about.

These things are the result of having the Spirit of Christ in you. Jesus didn't leave us defenseless when He went back to heaven. He gave us an arsenal of protection and tools for productivity. He gave us the Third Person of the Holy Trinity, the Holy Spirit, to lead us into all truth, be our comforter, and seal (protect) us until Christ comes back for us. Oh and by the way, the Bible says that we have the same power that raised Jesus from the dead inside of us. We have resurrection power inside of us!

Come on say it with me!

"That same power! That same power! That same power that raised Jesus from the dead lives in me! That same power. That same power!"

God's Armor of Protection

Speaking of protection. We have God himself dwelling within us, but He has also issued us spiritual armor.

This spiritual armor is described in Ephesians 6:11-17. This spiritual armor is for the believer, the follower of Christ.

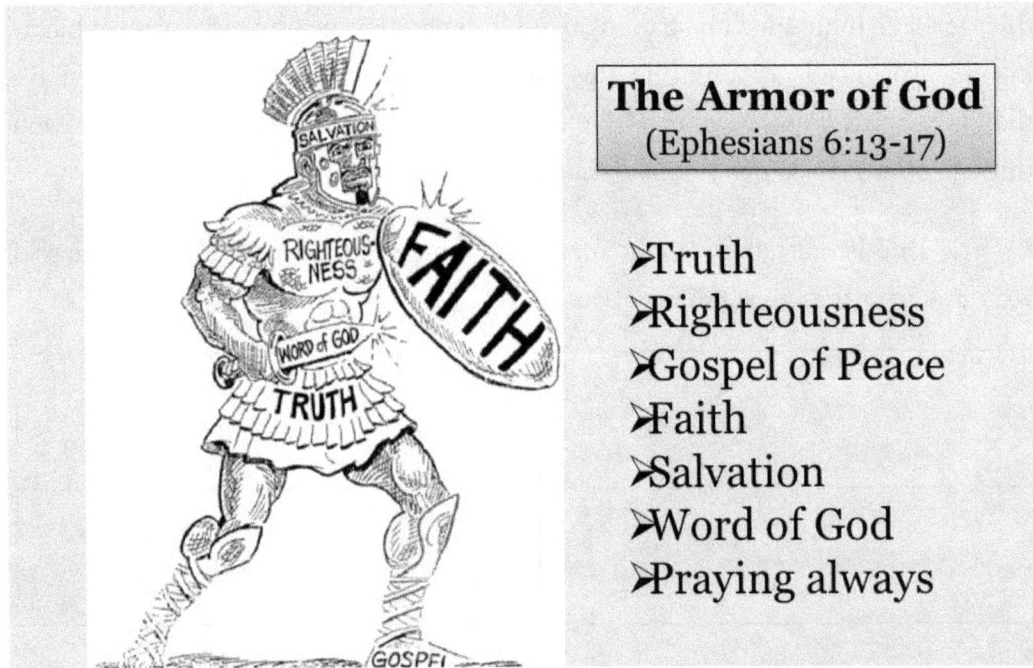

The Armor of God
(Ephesians 6:13-17)

➢Truth
➢Righteousness
➢Gospel of Peace
➢Faith
➢Salvation
➢Word of God
➢Praying always

There are various scriptures in the Bible that symbolize a believer and the Church. We are referred to as lambs, sheep, members of a body, a bride, a child, but we are also soldiers. Paul said that he had "fought the good fight of faith."

We are called to join the battle when we accept Christ as Savior and Lord. At the point of salvation, we are sealed with the Holy Spirit, and we become the righteousness of God in Christ. We are in Christ and Christ is in us. Does that stop the enemy from attacking us? Does that stop him from trying to draw our loyal hearts away from Christ? Absolutely not! The spiritual armor that we are to put on according to Ephesians 6:11-17 gives us an indication of the battle tactics of Satan. Try identifying what Satan tries to come against based upon each piece of armor.

Armor	What's protected?	What is attacked and why?
Helmet of Salvation		
Breastplate of Righteousness		
Belt of Truth		
Shield of Faith		
Sword of the Spirit (offensive weapon)	What is the purpose of the Sword of the Spirit?	
Shoes shod with the Gospel of Peace		

To guard our hearts is to guard the core of who we are. To fully protect the heart, we must fully guard our thoughts, affections, and our ear and eye gates. We need the spiritual gear of God to protect our minds in the truth that we have the mind of Christ and are the righteousness of God in Christ (1 Corinthians 2:16, 2 Corinthians 5:21). We need to know what the Bible says because it is the truth of God that we have been given to discern good from evil and to prove what the perfect will of God is (Romans 12:1-2). When we believe the Bible, we can quench the fiery darts of the enemy. The Bible calls this our shield of faith. Faith protects your heart, fear paralyzes it.

Satan loves to try and throw his messages of doubt, fear, and worry to our minds so that we are shaken. His tactic is to redirect our focus from God to ourselves. He wants us to depend on our efforts rather than trust God with our entire lives. When these darts of doubt come, we are to also take up the sword of the Spirit which is the Word of God and use the Word because it is alive and active. When we speak it out of our mouths it changes things. It accomplishes what God purposes it to do. Satan wants to muzzle us during our trials so that we don't speak the Word of God. Have you ever been so overwhelmed with emotions that it was hard to pray? Have you ever been so discouraged that it was nearly impossible to sing praises to God? Your heart has the ability to override your reasoning. Do not allow Satan to convince you to withhold your sacrifice of praise. Do not allow fear and discouragement to disarm the most powerful tool you have; prayer.

I have been in many situations where I was so depressed or anxious that I couldn't even pray. Reading scriptures out loud combats my feelings and any demonic influence because the Word of God divides between soul and spirit; remember? It divides what I'm feeling from truth; separating what is happening around me and what God is doing.

One aspect of our armor protects our spiritual feet. When the primary affection of your heart is Christ, your spiritual feet are operating at full capacity. Many people say their hearts belong to Jesus, but they refuse to go and tell others of their hearts' affection. The enemy loves to damper our affection for Christ so we forfeit the commission to, "Go". We should "shod" our feet with the Gospel of peace. We must always be prepared to give an answer for the hope that we have found in Christ. Why else would God leave you here on earth? Why didn't He just take you up to heaven as soon as you got saved? You still have a purpose to be His witness to those who do not know Jesus. God desires for everyone to be saved even though He knows there will be many that will reject Him to the very end. He still doesn't want anyone to perish (2 Peter 3:9).

Jesus said God sent Him and now He is sending us and that is an honor to be chosen by God to continue sharing the good news about Jesus. We get to participate in God's saving work! We have to put the gospel of peace on our feet and yield to God's leading of where to go and when to go. Even if He asks us to leave our hometown or our comfort zones; we are soldiers and that means we take our marching orders from the God of angel armies. You didn't just enter into God's family, you entered into God's kingdom; you're not just adopted as a child, you're chosen as His warrior.

I must decide daily whether or not I'm going to put on God's armor or put on what I like to call the world's wardrobe. Now this isn't in the Bible, but it really helps me to see the choices I can make each day, because I still live in a sinful world with a deceptive devil that loves to create the opposite of what God has designed. Remember, he comes to steal, kill, and destroy (John 10:10). He doesn't come in a way that is blatantly evil. He comes like a wolf in sheep's clothing or like an angel of light (2 Corinthians 11:14). He knows how to look the part, but he can't act the part. If you know the Word of God and have the Holy Spirit in you it is very possible to see through his disguises.

Below is the wardrobe of the world. Any of these look familiar? I have worn all of these at one point. Satan's sales pitch might sound something like, "Hey, these are so much lighter than that heavy armor. Wouldn't you rather fit in with your friends than to be rejected? You'll look like a clown in all that armor God wants you to wear. Put on these pieces and you'll be stylish, accepted, and happier."

Can you hear Satan now? Though these pieces look lightweight, they are much heavier than the armor God gives. Jesus says that His yoke is easy and His burden is light. His commandments are not burdensome. The armor of God makes our hearts beat with joy, love, power, and peace; but Satan's outfit only leaves us feeling heavy, burdened, guilty, depressed, unaccepted, unloved, weak, and anxious.

Let's go through and pinpoint any pieces we have that we want to repent of and ask God to remove and replace them with His armor.

Choose the Armor of God or the World's Wardrobe

				Which one do you have on? What thoughts do you have?
Helmet of Salvation	It is by grace through faith that I'm saved not by my works or else I could take the credit. I think about the finish work of Jesus Christ on the cross and my hope and trust is Him for the cleansing of my sins.	Fitted cap of Fear	I don't try because I'm afraid of failure, being rejected, being misunderstood. I fear that I will never be good enough so why even try?	
Breastplate of Righteousness	I am the righteousness of God in Christ Jesus so I choose not to live in regrets. There is no condemnation so I am free to fully obey God and live a life of service and worship to Him.	T-shirt of regrets	I should have…. could have…. would have…. It is too late now…if only they wouldn't have…. if only I would have had….	
Belt of Truth	Jesus is the way, the truth, the life and I will learn and study the Bible so my mind can be renewed and I can be transformed so my actions and affections will align with His will.	Lace of Lusts	Truth is what I say it is. If I want it I'm going to get it, if I need it then it's my responsibility to make it happen. I'm not going to let anyone outdo me. I'm self-reliant, independent, and my happiness is priority.	

Shield of Faith	My belief in what God says protects me and sets me on right paths. I will believe God even if people say something different. I choose to live my life by my faith in God not by what I see or understand.	Face of falsehood	I protect my heart by putting on a mask and letting people see only what I want them to see. My decisions in life are based not who God says I am, but what other people want me to be. I choose to walk by what I see.	
Sword of the Spirit	I am a skilled workman of God, studying God's Word so that I can correctly handle (share and live) by what it says. I don't just hear the Word, but I live the Word. I patiently yield to the Holy Spirit; letting Him lead me into all truth.	Dagger of sinful flesh	I don't like to read. I don't understand the Bible. I don't like to wait. Waiting on God is a waste of time. Whatever I desire I go for. Sometimes I make choices that God isn't pleased with. I'm only human. God understands.	
Shoes shod with the preparation of the Gospel of Peace	I am not ashamed of the Gospel of Jesus Christ because it is the power of God for salvation to everyone who believes. Here I am God, you can send me to share your good news to those who need to hear. I'm ready.	Heels of self will / Steel boots of stubbornness	God may ask me to go or do something that I just don't want to. Telling people about Jesus is just not for me. They'll hear from someone else. I just can't go. I just won't go. I'd rather just do my own thing. At least I'm saved and not going to hell.	

Your quotes may be different from the ones provided. Your thinking may be different. The blank column is for you to identify what you have on and write down the thoughts that you have that would confirm which article of clothing you have on.

The Restored Heart

The thing I love about God is that He loves to take wrongs and make them right. My grandfather says, "He specializes in things impossible; he can do what no other power can do."

1 John 1:9 puts it like this, "If you confess your sins He is faithful and just to forgive you of all your sins and cleanse you from all unrighteousness."

It's amazing that God sees the wax on your heart, but He patiently waits until you confess it to Him. Sometimes we don't really know it's there, so He reveals it by His Spirit and His Word. Once we identify it and stop in our tracks. He doesn't just forgive us, but He cleanses us. He removes the wax.

In the armor exercise, did you identify some wrong thoughts and even some sins that you need to stop? I know I did and I have. Now, you can always pray out of the honesty of your heart, but this is a similar prayer to the one I prayed.

Father,

Thank You that You showed me my wrong thinking. I want to thank You that You showed me where I have traded in the powerful armor You have given me for the convenient, but very costly outfit of the world. I repent right now and I denounce this way of thinking and believing. I take every thought captive that tries to exalt itself against the knowledge of You. I thank You for forgiving me, but that's not all. I need You to empower me by Your Spirit to take off the clothing of the world and put on the armor of God. I want to take off_____ and put on _____. I can do all things through Christ who strengthens me. Empower me to follow through on this decision to daily put on the whole armor of God. Keep me from the enticing lace of lust that looks so beautiful. The pretty lace makes me think I need what the world offers in order to be beautiful or to be of any value. I take it off now! I put on the Belt of Truth that says I am fearfully and wonderfully made by You. I am made in Your image and it doesn't get any more beautiful than that. I take off _____ now, and I put on _____ in its place so that having done all to stand; I can continue to stand. Thank you Father and it's in Jesus name I pray this prayer.

Amen

Let the safe on the cover of the book remind you that your eternal safety comes from placing your faith and trust in Jesus Christ. Jesus died for the sins of the world, but in order for His blood to be applied to your heart you must believe (Romans 10:9, John 3:16). Your faith opens the door of the safe where you can place your heart. Once your heart is in the safe, let the crown and the cross remind you that your life is hidden in Christ and Christ's life is in you. Though you bear your cross for Christ in this life, He has an eternal crown waiting for you when He returns. Let it remind you that Christ is your first love and you are His.

We have walked through a security plan to help you maintain your passion and affection for Christ. God promises in Romans 8:38 that nothing can separate you from His love, so my prayer is that this book has encouraged you to let nothing separate God from your love.

TAKE IT TO HEART

Take a moment and reflect on all you have read. Answering these questions will help you to recapture many of the things we have discussed.

♥ Have you asked Jesus Christ into your heart?

♥ Is He your first love?

♥ Is there a breach in your security? If so, in what area? (entrance, lockers, lobby, or holding area)

♥ How will you take off the "world's wardrobe"?

♥ How will you put on the Armor of God?

♥ What is distracting you from meeting God in your secret chamber?

♥ Who will you put on your security list to encourage you in your faith?

♥ Who can you confide in to confess your sins and encourage you in God's Word?

♥ What are the things you need to take in the throne room and lay at Christ's feet?

♥ What other affections of your heart do you need to trust Jesus with?

♥ How can you actively share your heart's affection for Christ?

My friend,

Thank you for sharing in this journey with me, *and [may] the peace of God, which surpasses all understanding, guard your hearts and your minds in Christ Jesus (Philippians 4:7).*

References

"Affection." *Merriam-Webster Dictionary, 1828. Merriam-Webster.com.* https://www.merriam-webster.com/dictionary/affection

Kohler, Kaufman, et.al. "Heart." Jewish Encyclopedia. 22 Jan. 2016, www.jewishencyclopedia.com/articles/7436-heart.

Parsons, John J. "Keep thy Heart." Hebrews 4 Christians, 22 Jan. 2016, www.hebrew4christians.com/Meditations/Keep_thy_heart/ keep_thy_heart.html.

Answer Key

NOTE. Some questions are not answered here. Pray for the answers to questions that may not have a definite answer. Remember, whatever the answer, it should always be affirmed by scripture.

God Who Sees: Genesis 16

Who was Hagar?
(16:1) Sarai's Egyptian servant

Why did Hagar run away?
(16:4-6) Sarai was jealous because she was barren and Hagar got pregnant with Abram's baby. Even though it was Sarai's idea, she treated Hagar harshly and Hagar fled.

Who did Hagar meet as she was fleeing?
(16:7) The angel (messenger) of the LORD.

What was the message from this visitor? (16:9-12)

1. Return to your mistress and submit to her

2. "I will surely multiply your offspring so that they cannot be numbered for multitude."

3. It's a boy! His name was to be called Ishmael

4. The LORD listened to her affliction

5. Her son would be wild. He would be against everyone and everyone against him. He would dwell over all his kinsmen

What was Hagar's response?
(16:3) "You are a God of seeing…. truly here I have seen him who looks after me."

What name did Hagar give to God?

(16:3) God of seeing; El Roi

Gaining or Regaining Security: John 6:1-21 pg. 62

Why were so many people following Jesus?
(6:2) Because they saw the signs of healing He was doing on sick people.

When Jesus looked up and saw a huge number of people coming towards Him what question did He ask Philip?
(6:5) "Where are we to buy bread, so that these people may eat?"

Did He ask the question because He didn't know the answer? How do you know?
(6:6) No. Scripture says, "He did this to test him, for He Himself knew what He would do."

What was the only solution the disciples could come up with for this dilemma?
(6:7-8) Philip gave no solution. He only acknowledged the magnitude of the problem, but Andrew suggested a boy's fish and loaves.

What did Jesus ask the people to do?
(6:10) He asked the disciples to have the people sit down.

How many men were there?
(6:10) 5,000 men

What did Jesus do with the food that was given Him by the young boy?
(6:11) Took them, gave thanks for them, and distributed them

Verse 15: Why did Jesus leave and go up to the mountain? Why didn't He want the people to crown Him King when He is King? (John 5:24, 41-47; Matthew 20:28)
John 5:41 "I do not receive glory from people."
Matthew 20:28 Jesus came to serve not to be served, and give His life for many.

Verses 16-21, pgs. 64-65

Why were the disciples in a boat on the sea?

Jesus told them to get into the boat and go ahead of Him to the other side.

What happened while they were at sea?

A rough storm came (v. 18).

Why were they afraid?

They saw Jesus walking on the sea (v. 19).

What security did they find in letting Jesus in the boat and what happened to their boat after they willingly let Jesus in?

As soon as they let Jesus in the boat they immediately found themselves on the other side (v. 21).

Answers to Chart on page 66

Use the remainder of the chart to fill in the roles that Jesus has and how He is FOR us and AGAINST sin and Satan.

Revelations 1:8, 17-18 Jesus is the Alpha and Omega, "Who is, and who was, and who is to come, the Almighty."	John 10:9 I Am the _____gate_____	John 10:14 I Am the ___Good_____ ____Shepherd_____
Job 19:25 My ____ **Redeemer**_____ Lives!	Luke 2:11 A _____Savior_____ is given!	Hebrews 3:1 **The_Apostle_and_High_ Priest__**
Isaiah 9:6 (a lot of names here!) **Wonderful Counselor Mighty God Everlasting Father Prince of Peace**	John 8:58 ___I AM_____	John 1:29 ___Lamb of God_____

Hebrews 12:2	Psalm 18:2	Proverbs 21:31
__Author/Perfector of our_Faith____	___Rock, Fortress, Deliverer__	__Victory__ belongs to the LORD.

Answer for chart on pg. 67

Apostle Paul is not talking about apples and oranges here. Read this scripture and write the fruit that he is talking about.

Love	Peace
Kindness	Faithfulness
Joy	Patience
Goodness	Gentleness
	Self-control

Partners' Page

This space is a platform for my partners to share their "heart stories" with you. Feel free to contact them for any of their services. Thank you Partners for assisting me in getting this message out. Your talents, professionalism, and support made this project more enjoyable.

Jesus Christ is the love of my life because I am the love of His. He cares enough about me and those like me—the poor, the weak, the fallen—to offer us salvation and redemption through His atoning sacrifice on the cross. He is the Great Artist, imbuing His creation with the utmost subtlety and beauty, and through His Holy Spirit, He allows us—His creation—to experience His glory by creating things ourselves. Where we would have false alarm, He grants us true calm. There is no good and no love apart from Him, for He is good and He is love.

Patrick Ragland
Writer, Editor, and Musician
anaphorist@gmail.com
soundcloud.com/patrick-ragland

Our Testimony: David & Jennifer Mason —
Founders of Agape Ambassadors Inc.

"Jesus is our Savior and our Healer. He has healed both of us from life-threatening diseases and shown us how real He is so we can "go tell" troubled youth that Jesus is worthy of their trust, God's Word is truth, and their need of unconditional "agape" love can only be filled by receiving Jesus as Savior and Lord. He has provided for us in supernatural ways. He has graced us with two beautiful children, David Jr. and Jessica- who love and

serve Him – one of whom authored this book. Our response to all this outpouring of His grace is to love Him with all our hearts, minds, bodies, and souls; to worship Him in fulfilling His call on our lives to be Agape Ambassadors according to His Word. (2 Corinthians 5:20)

David & Jennifer, along with Jessica and "DJ" are privileged to lead an awesome team in providing annual retreats for kids in Juvenile Detention facilities. These retreats are called "Jesus is the Answer", and involve volunteers from local churches. Many students have given their lives to Christ since retreats started in 2000. EVERYONE EXPERIENCES GOD'S POWERFUL PRESENCE & WATCH HIM MIRACULOUSLY TRANSFORM LIVES RIGHT BEFORE THEIR VERY EYES!!! HEARTS & LIVES ARE CHANGED FOREVER!!

In addition to the retreats, the ministry mentor youth from Lynchburg Detention Center Post Programs and Group Homes. They provide life skills, enrichment programs, career counseling and discipleship with the help of community volunteers. We try to help the students make a beneficial plan for their future. Agape Ambassadors Inc. is a 501(c)3 non-profit ministry and operates solely on donations.

The ministry welcomes your support, prayers, and donations.

Services this ministry provides include:

♥ JESUS IS THE ANSWER RETREATS in 3 of our local detention homes. Our desire is to include more facilities as the resources & volunteer base grows and we can get volunteers from the community around the additional facilities we travel to serve. Commitment to the training and at least 1 whole day of service for each of the 3 retreat days is needed.

♥ COMING SOON: "Retreats on the Outside" for teens in churches, group homes, Sweet Meet (Teen and Mom Mentorship), etc.

♥ Minister David is a DYNAMIC motivational speaker for youth groups. At age 19, God saved him from a rebellious lifestyle. When He shares, youth are captivated and inspired. He is also willing to speak to various ministries and churches about the retreats and how they can help. For information about any of these services or outreach opportunities, please feel free to contact the ministry.

Agape Ambassadors Inc.
P.O. Box 2028
Forest, VA 24551
agapeambassadors@verizon.net
Agape Ambassadors Inc (Facebook)

Sweet Meet Ministries

Sweet Meet is a ministry under Agape Ambassadors Inc. that strives to support mothers and their teen daughters to plug into the "sweet" presence of Christ Jesus together. The anthem scripture is 1 Peter 2:9,

"But you are a chosen race, a royal priesthood, a holy nation, a people for his own possession, that you may proclaim the excellencies of him who called you out of darkness into his marvelous light."

Sweet Meet celebrates the beauty of being a godly woman, a royal daughter of the Almighty God, and a witness of Christ's ultimate sacrifice for our sins. Considering these truths, we address each other with royal titles. Our mentors are called "Queens", our mothers are called "Duchesses", and our teens are called "Princesses. We have seen relationships restored, truth revealed, faith strengthened, and the presence of God infiltrate communities. Sweet Meet emphasizes the satisfying and enjoyable experience of meeting the presence of Jesus Christ, through the Word of God, with women of all ages.

For more information about Sweet Meet you can contact Jessica at Guardmyheart4u@gmail.com

*Special thanks to Carmela and Rising Sun Missionary for your love, support, and participation in Sweet Meet as our primary partner. Words will never express how grateful I am for friends and prayer warriors like you!

Jesus is my everything. He keeps me every day, and provides my every need. He hears me when I call on His name. I know the power of His Word and prayer. If He never does another thing for me, I still know that He is the Truth, the Way and the Life. Each new day is just the beginning with God if we only believe!

I am thankful that I met Jessica, to hear her testimony and privileged to be able to help her with this book.

Nonie Ratcliff
Pen to Print Publishing Services
nonierat123@gmail.com

www.ingramcontent.com/pod-product-compliance
Lightning Source LLC
LaVergne TN
LVHW081328060426
835513LV00012B/1228